Choosing the Gift
of Forgiveness

Choosing the Gift of Forgiveness

How to Overcome Hurts and Brokenness

Robert W. Harvey and David G. Benner

Strategic Christian Living Series

Baker Books

A Division of Baker Book House Co
Grand Rapids, Michigan 49516

Published by Baker Books
a division of Baker Book House Company
P.O. Box 6287, Grand Rapids, MI 49516-6287

Printed in the United States of America

Library of Congress Cataloging-in-Publication Data

Harvey, Robert W.
    Choosing the gift of forgiveness: how to overcome hurts and brokenness / Robert W. Harvey and David G. Benner.
        p.   cm.—(Strategic Christian living series)
    Includes bibliographical references
    ISBN 0-8010-5656-X (paper)
        1. Forgiveness—religious aspects—Christianity. I. Benner, David G. II. Title. III. Series: Strategic Christian living.
    BV4647.F55H36 1996
    234'.5—dc20   96-11812

Other Books in the Strategic Christian Living Series

CONTENTS

1

The Importance of Forgiveness

The most important single concept in Christianity is that of forgiveness. Christianity is a religion of good news and that good news is that in Christ our sins are forgiven and that makes it possible for us to forgive others for their sins against us. Throughout both Old and New Testaments we are presented with the supreme value of forgiveness. In fact, it is presented as a prospect so desirable that it seems to loom as the most essential experience for wholeness in life. Consider some of the vivid images with which biblical authors portray the blessing of receiving God's forgiving grace.

Forgiveness produces:

A sense of cleanness: David prays longingly, "Wash away all my iniquity and cleanse me from my sin . . . cleanse me . . . and I will be clean, wash me, and I will be whiter than snow" (Ps. 51:2, 7). God counters Satan's accusations against Joshua the high priest by commanding that Joshua's filthy clothes (symbolic of sin) be removed by an angel and clean clothes be given to him, saying, "See, I have taken away your sin . . ." (Zech. 3:1–5).

A sense of guilt decisively removed: King Hezekiah felt the authority with which God had declared him forgiven, "You have put all my sins behind your back" (Isa. 38:17). The prophet Micah anticipated God's thorough removal of guilt, "Who is a God like you, who pardons sin and forgives . . . You will tread our sins underfoot and hurl all our iniquities into the depths of the sea" (Micah 7:18–19). God declared his power to remove sin's condemnation to Israel. "I have swept away your offenses like a cloud, your sins like the morning mist" (Isa. 44:22).

A sense of healing and emotional release: "But for you who revere my name, the sun of righteousness will rise with healing in its wings. And you will go out and leap like calves released from the stall" (Mal. 4:2).

A new clarity of mind about God's purpose: "I pray also that the eyes of your heart may be enlightened in order that you may know the hope to which he has called you, the riches of his glorious inheritance in the saints, and his incomparably great power for us who believe" (Eph. 1:18–19).

A new unity between persons: "How good and pleasant it is when brothers dwell together in unity! It is like precious oil poured on the head, running down . . . It is like the dew. . . ." (Ps. 133). Reconciled persons experience the pleasure of new beginnings ("dew") and new attractiveness to one another (sweet smelling, glistening oil in the hair).

Forgiveness is a freeing, empowering, refreshing, healing, and joyful experience which is capable of transforming all of life. Therefore, the failure to forgive or be forgiven means the loss of much or all of this emotional health from one's experience. This tragic cost of the failure of forgiveness is also graphically portrayed in Scripture.

An absence of forgiveness produces:

A *clinging sense of uncleanness and lostness:* ". . . all our righteous acts are like filthy rags; we all shrivel up like a leaf and like the wind our sins sweep us away" (Isa. 64:6).

A *sense of unresolved guilt:* ". . . my sin is always before me" (Ps. 51:3).

A *continuing sense of woundedness and longing for healing:* "I am feeble and utterly crushed; I groan in anguish of heart" (Ps. 38:8). "Let me hear joy and gladness; let the bones you have crushed rejoice" (Ps. 51:8).

Darkness of mind and confusion about God's purpose: "He feeds on ashes, a deluded heart misleads him . . . We look for light, but all is darkness; for brightness, but we walk in deep shadows. Like the blind we grope along the wall . . . at midday we stumble . . ." (Isa. 44:20; 59:9–10).

A *growing disunity between persons:* even within the Christian fellowship: "If you keep biting and devouring each other, watch out or you will be destroyed by each other" (Gal. 5:15).

Forgiveness and Health

The process of confession, repentance, and forgiveness is at the core of the Christian model of healing of our alienation from both God and each other. But forgiveness involves even more than the healing of our relationships. Scripture also presents evidence for a link between forgiveness and health. David spoke of his "bones wasting away" and his "strength being sapped" until he finally confessed his sins and received God's forgiveness (Ps. 32:3–4). Similar symptoms appear to be his experience connected to guilt in Psalm 38: "My guilt overwhelmed me . . . My back is filled with searing pain; there is no health in my body . . . My heart pounds, my strength fails me. . . ." (vv. 4, 7, 10). Jesus also demonstrated the close connection between forgiveness and physical health in his cure of the paralytic who was healed as a result of Jesus forgiving his sin (Matt. 9:1–8).

This close connection between forgiveness and health has also been noted by medical researchers. Recent research has shown that the experience of receiving forgiveness strengthens the body's immune system and helps us ward off or heal more rapidly from disease. On the other hand, people who have a tendency to hold resentment and a related inability to forgive others are much more likely to develop a range of diseases, including cancer and heart disease. An even more direct risk to physical life has been noted by psychiatrist E. Mansell Pattison, who suggests that murder typifies the ultimate failure to forgive another, and suicide, the ultimate failure to forgive oneself. A failure to forgive others, and the accompanying resentment and bitterness, has also been reported to be the number one cause of burnout.

In the light of the destructiveness of resentment and the healing nature of forgiveness, it is important that we forgive others for their offenses against us as quickly as possible. Resentment is a poison that destroys our body, soul, and spirit, and we should, therefore, strive to neutralize this poison with the antidote of forgiveness as soon as possible. Forgiveness is an unmerited gift through the sacrificial atonement accomplished by Jesus Christ. It is God's offer of health and wholeness.

Forgiveness as the Remedy for Injustice

Perhaps the best news about forgiveness is that it and it alone offers to break the bondage of the hurts of our past. The Jewish philosopher, Hannah Arendt, states that "The only remedy for the inevitability of our history is forgiveness." Bad things will inevitably happen to us. But we do not have to be victims of those events. Forgiveness offers us the possibility of freedom from the bondage to the past.

There is no denying the fact that life can be cruel. Few people, if any, fail to experience unjust, unfair things which they in no way deserve. Children are physically and sexually abused by those entrusted with their care. Employees are exploited by unjust employers and employers are cheated by dishonest employees. Every day women and children continue to be victimized by abusive males. Husbands and wives are betrayed by unfaithful spouses. And friends are betrayed by those they thought to be their friends.

While there is no denying the fact that these things are unfair, it would be even more unfair if we were forced to be victims of the bad things that happen to us. To state that forgiveness offers the possibility of release from such victimization is not to suggest that forgiveness is easy or that the pain of emotional wounds associated with betrayal of trust will not be very real. Such pain is acute and at times almost unbelievably intense. But we do not have to be tyrannized by these hurts for the rest of our lives. Forgiveness is the offer of freedom and healing from the hurts which we receive but don't deserve.

Much of our lives are beyond our control. And once experiences have occurred, there is nothing we can do to change them. This is why we often view ourselves as victims, victimized by the uncontrollable. But while we cannot control what happens to us, we can choose how we react to these things. We cannot change our history but we can, through forgiveness, experience healing and even growth from the hurtful things which we experience.

Coping with Life's Disappointments

The Old Testament patriarch Job knew hurts and disappointments. In fact, so regularly did life and disappointment go together that he concluded that "Man is born to trouble as surely as sparks fly upward" (Job 5:7).

The common component in the diverse list of things that can and do go wrong is that life does not turn out as hoped. Not always is it immediately obvious to us that we have, in fact, been operating with expectations which are now disappointed. However, our reactions betray an underlying expectation. On reflection, this expectation may be seen to be totally unrealistic (such as, "I expect to live in good health forever," or, "I expect my son to be like me") or it may be more reasonable (such as, "I expect my friends to always treat me with respect," or, "I expect my husband to remain faithful to me"). But either consciously or subconsciously we do have expectations about our lives, and our reactions to life's disappointments can in one sense be understood as reactions to these expectations.

The manner in which a person reacts to an experience of life which has not turned out as hoped for depends on a great variety of factors. One of these is the nature of the expectation. Expectations vary on a continuum from demand to hope. At the demand end of this continuum, the expected experience is viewed as an inalienable right. At the hope end, the expected experience is viewed as more of a wished for outcome. People tend to respond to expectations of the "demand" variety primarily with anger. In contrast, they more typically respond to expectations of the "hope" variety with sadness. Since most expectations contain elements of both these forms of anticipation, it is most common for people to respond to disappointments with a mixture of both anger and sadness. Whether these disappointments take the form of disappointment with others or with self, the central dynamic in the redemptive and healing process will always be forgiveness.

The major cause of emotional wounds is disappointment with others. Whether it be an unfaithful husband or one who seems to love his work more than his family, a wife who has lost her faith and has become cynical of anything to do with religion, a business partner whose behaviors seem to violate the basic values and agreements of the partnership, a close friend who appears to have forgotten the friendship, or a child who is alienated from the family, the feeling of disappointment with others is in each case the core of the experienced hurt.

But as noted above, the emotional response to disappointment is highly variable. Because of this it is not always clear that the underlying experience is one of disappointment. Sadness, the core feeling in most people's response to disappointment, may be masked by anger, and it, in turn, may be masked by chronic suspiciousness, jealousy, self-pity, impatience, cynicism, or depression. Usually at the root of these feelings and behaviors, one can find a sense of having been disappointed in a relationship and it is this core experience which usually must be resolved in order to experience healing of the emotional wounds.

Disappointment in another person is usually experienced as a violation of a trust. An unfaithful spouse or an unjust employer are both perceived as violating an implicit contract, a contract which specified, among other things, fairness and fidelity. We feel hurt when others do not play by the rules of these implicit contracts because we trust that others will treat us fairly. As C. S. Lewis notes, even the most thorough-going ethical relativist who disavows any external reference point for morality quickly discovers the operation of internal standards of morality the moment these are violated by the behavior of another.

Resolution of the feelings which tend to mask emotional injury is extremely difficult without identifying the underlying sense of disappointment because without such an identification, forgiveness seems irrelevant. What sense does it make to speak of forgiveness in relation to depression, self-pity, chronic suspiciousness, or jealousy? Without recognizing that at core I am angry at someone whom

I perceive to have trampled over my rights and violated a trust (either implicit or explicit), I am left stuck with that anger. Forgiveness of another person becomes relevant only when I recognize that there is another person who needs my forgiveness.

Sometimes the person we are disappointed with is God. The fact that life is unfair may lead us to conclude that God is unfair. For the Christian, such feelings are usually quite confusing. Is it appropriate to be angry at God? And, is it meaningful to speak of forgiving God? But underneath these questions is an even more basic one, Where is God when we experience the obvious unfairness of life?

In his book *Disappointment with God,* Philip Yancey suggests that the feelings of anger at God reflect a confusion of God and life.[1] There is no question, he suggests, that life is unfair. But where is God when these things happen? Yancey's answer is that God is in us as we experience these injustices. God is not behind these disasters in life. Rather he stands with us, sharing our anger, hurt, despair, and pain.

Another way of answering this question, "Where is God when I am being hurt?" is to note that at such times, and at all times God is in Jesus hanging on the cross. In other words, when I suffer, so does the Eternal Suffering Servant. I cannot experience any suffering that is unknown to God. Jesus knows suffering. Our God is not above or beyond suffering. Jesus suffered and died for us. The Christian God knows suffering and seeks to redeem it and us through it.

Finally, sometimes our disappointment is with ourself. Forgiveness of one's self is often much more difficult than forgiveness of others. While related to forgiving others, it raises some unique challenges.

At the core of the challenge of forgiving others is anger, my anger at them for what they did to me. On the other hand, at the core of the challenge of forgiving myself is guilt, my guilt over having done what I should not have done, or not done what I should have. Both anger and guilt are forms of bondage to the past and the remedy for both is forgiveness. Release from both is based on the experience of having been forgiven. However, the challenge of dealing with guilt is different enough from that of dealing with anger that it will be dealt with separately, briefly in chapter 4 where we will consider the reasons why it is often so difficult to forgive ourselves, and at more length in chapter 6 where we will examine the role of grace in experiencing freedom from guilt and genuine forgiveness of ourselves.

Forgiveness as a Hard-Work Miracle

While forgiveness involves great effort, these efforts do not produce forgiveness. Forgiveness is something that we do by a free act of our will, but the ability to forgive is a gift, we might even say a miracle.

This should not be understood as in any way minimizing the effort that is required. As noted by David Augsburger, "True forgiveness is the hardest thing in the universe." No human action is more difficult than genuine forgiveness. Nothing more difficult will ever be asked of any human than to forgive someone who hurt them. However, the release of anger and the healing of damaged emotions that comes from forgiveness is not something that I produce by my efforts. I do the hard work that is my part and then I receive the wonderful gift of forgiveness. It is something, therefore, that I should receive with gratitude.

Forgiveness requires that we do our part and then we ask God to do his part. His part is in helping us release the anger and then in giving us the resulting emotional freedom and healing. I don't simply pray to God that he will render the other person forgiven by me. Unfortunately it is not that easy. But I can and should pray that God would help me forgive the other person. This is a prayer he will answer because it is clearly something that he wills for me.

But it is here that we need to note the relationship between receiving forgiveness and giving it. As it is hard to imagine how one could ever give love if he or she had never received love from another, so, too, it is hard to imagine how someone could forgive another if he or she had never received forgiveness themselves. Knowing myself to be one who has needed and received forgiveness allows me to grant others this great and undeserved gift. And supremely, knowing myself to have needed and received the forgiveness of God allows me to become a forgiving person in a way that is quite impossible when only dealing with the experience of forgiveness as received from the hands of fellow humans. "God's forgiveness toward me and my forgiveness toward another are like the voice and the echo."[2] Without the former, the latter is both impossible and a meaningless absurdity.

Forgiveness is always a gift, a grace. I become capable of giving forgiveness because I have already received it. I didn't have to earn it from those who gave it to me and similarly, those who hurt me can do nothing to earn it from me. Forgiveness is, in essence, a gift of unearned extravagance and generosity.

Nothing in the world bears the impression of the Son of God so clearly as forgiveness. Jesus Christ, the incarnate Son of God, is the greatest miracle of all possible miracles. He is the wondrous gracious coming of God himself to us to rescue us from guilt and death and bestow upon us the incomparable gift of new life, present and eternal. We may reverently say that the incarnation is a miracle even beyond that of the creation when God spoke a word and the universe sprang into existence (2 Peter 3:5). We may also say that the work he accomplished, the work of redemption, was a work of difficulty beyond any ever conceived in history (Isa. 63:3; Heb. 9:9, 14). If, in our human experience, we are able to forgive "as in Christ God forgave" us (Eph. 4:32), then our acts of forgiveness will bear the impression of the Great Forgiver—they will be both miraculous and difficult. They will be indeed "hard-work miracles."

But often we tend to believe in the hard work of forgiveness more than we believe in or expect it as a miracle of grace. It is so hard to trust that you have truly been forgiven. When you have harmed someone and have repented of the wrong you have done; when you ache with regret and beg for their pardon; when you long for things to be again as they were before your offense, but suspect that they can never be so; then part of you despairs that full forgiveness can, in reality, ever be given to you.

> When you deal intimately with human beings . . . you wonder at times if forgiveness is not as rare as hen's teeth. People bury hatchets but carefully tuck away the map which tells where their hidden weapon lies. We put our resentments in cold storage and then pull the switch to let them thaw out again. Our grudges are taken out to the lake to drown them—even the lake of prayer—and we end up giving them a swimming lesson. How often we have torn up the cancelled note but hang on to the wastebasket that holds the pieces. This is not to say that human forgiveness does not occur; only that it is rare and that much that passes for forgiveness is often not so at all.[3]

The Promise of Forgiveness

As unfamiliar or uneasy as we may be with forgiveness, we are certainly well acquainted with disappointment; it is basic to our emotional pain when others hurt or fail us. The Bible that so confidently proclaims the miracle of forgiveness also unhesitatingly faces up to the realities of disappointment. The Scripture is utterly familiar with and sympathetic to the experiences that make it hard for us to be forgiving, recording faithfully the complaints of persons shocked, amazed, or saddened by the pain of injustice.

Job only needs to hear the theologically correct but accusing speech of one of his friends to begin to feel abandoned and to complain, "A despairing man should have the devotion of his friends . . . but my brothers are as undependable as intermittent streams . . . (where) caravans . . . look for water . . . only to be disappointed" (Job 6:14–20).

David, suffering the malice of his enemies, finds it most bitter that "Even my close friend, whom I trusted, he who shared my bread, has lifted up his heel against me" (Ps. 41:9).

And even Jesus who "knew what was in man," seems to speak in tones of disappointment when disciples desert, "You do not want to leave too, do you?" (John 6:67) and the closest of his friends fail him at his most vulnerable moment, "Could you men not keep watch with me for one hour?" (Matt. 26:38–40).

In the face of such persistent honesty about the pervasive experience of being victimized and disappointed, the Scripture, nevertheless, exuberantly proclaims the importance and wonders of forgiveness, both as it is offered to us and as we are enabled to offer it to others. Let us consider two examples.

Some Bible interpreters have commented that the first book of the Bible closes with words which ironically mark the predicament of humankind because of the fall into sin and its penalty, death: ". . . in a coffin in Egypt" (Gen. 50:26). But that final page of the Bible's opening document also records an incident that poignantly prepares us for the answer of God to our sin and death, the answer that is central to Scripture and crucial to redeemed human relationships: forgiveness.[4]

Genesis 50:15–21

When Joseph's brothers saw that their father was dead, they said, "What if Joseph holds a grudge against us and pays us back for all the wrongs we did to him?" So they sent word to Joseph, saying, "Your father left these instructions before he died: 'This is what you are to say to Joseph: I ask you to forgive your brothers the sins and the wrongs they committed in treating you so badly.' Now please forgive the sins of the servants of the God of your father." When their message came to him, Joseph wept.

His brothers then came and threw themselves down before him. "We are your slaves," they said. But Joseph said to them, "Don't be afraid. Am I in the place of God? You intended to harm me, but God intended it for good to accomplish what is now being done, the saving of many lives. So then, don't be afraid. I will provide for you and your children." And he reassured them and spoke kindly to them.

In Joseph's encounter with his brothers we discover several elements in the importance and power of forgiveness. To begin with, Joseph does not belittle the heinousness of his brothers' actions. Forgiveness takes brokenness seriously and affirms that guilt is real, but also affirms that guilt is not the last word. While agreeing with his brothers' confession of responsibility for his suffering, Joseph opens the way to new beginnings in their relationships with him (vv. 20–21, "you intended to harm me, but . . . don't be afraid"). Again, we should observe that Joseph seems to see through and beyond his brothers' clumsy attempt to manipulate his sympathy with a fictitious message in his father's name (vv. 16–17) and understand some of their feelings of fear and mistrust. Certainly his weeping (v. 17) is because at last they admit their wrong and ask his forgiveness, but also because he is now able to relinquish both the roles of victim and of judge (v. 19, "Am I in the place of God?") and see himself as "more like than unlike" the persons who have hurt him. That ability is evidence of Joseph's own progress in healing from the emotional wounds suffered in his brothers' cruelties. With God's help he has been "rewriting" his memories and realizing that his recall of painful events is not the whole picture of his life. He sees God's providence even in his brothers' malice and is able to think beyond the consequences for himself and be glad that his suffering led to "the saving of many lives" (v. 20). Joseph is now willing to leave the past alone and turn away from wounded retribution. He may not be able to resolve in his thinking all the reasons for the pain that overtook him, but he can accept the ambiguity, see the overcoming hand of God, and be free of bondage to the past. In this way, forgiveness gives freedom from the past and from its pain.

Joseph's brothers show a common misunderstanding of the nature of forgiveness as they attempt to negotiate a new standing with Joseph (v. 18, "We are your slaves"). This may be partly a culturally conventional way of speaking to one in the high position of power now enjoyed by their brother, but certainly both Joseph and the brothers are aware that he is, in fact, exactly in position to make his mercy to them part of a contract whereby they pay for their guilt with some form of bondage.

But forgiveness shuns such "contracts," in favor of the boundless possibilities it hopes for in the vitality of grace. Wherever interpersonal relationships are dominated by contracts, both the individual and their relationships are diminished. Joseph will not consider having such power over his brothers; he opts rather for the power of free forgiveness enabled by his God.

Contractual kinds of agreements about behavior between the perpetrator and the victim can fashion a kind of fairness and "just deserts" solution to broken relationships, but it is an impersonal solution that heals superficially. So far does the power of forgiveness take Joseph beyond the need of such manipulated control that he is able to give blessing instead of exacting tribute! (Verse 21, "So then, don't be afraid, I will provide for you and your children.") In the Hebrew, the "I" is emphatic, telling us that Joseph is promising something more than official philanthropy; he is determined to be personally involved in the lives of their families for ongoing good and filial caring. As Lyman Lundeen observes, "Forgiveness is an initiative that liberates individuals without the loss of relationships. It asserts openness in the face of the momentum of past decisions; instead of isolating victims and oppressors, it opens the way to new beginnings . . . In the end, the kind of liberation forgiveness offers ties us together rather than separates us . . . Forgiveness changes the entire situation for individuals. It frees them to be themselves—together . . . Forgiveness can sustain the drive for greater fairness, but it does so by going beyond it."[5]

Finally, we see that Joseph's forgiveness is very much grounded in his faith in God's living presence. Just how real God and his grace are to the brothers may be hard to discern with certainty. Their appeal to common faith and covenantal solidarity (v. 17, "Now please forgive the sins of the servants of the God of your father") may be suspect as yet another manipulative strategy. But the vital factor in this story of the importance of forgiveness is that Joseph at least clearly links God's grace to his own reasons for forgiving (vv. 19–20). Thus we are confronted with the miracle part of the hard-work miracle! Those we forgive may be neither adequately repentant nor ready to be honest with us in all parts of our future relationship, but by the grace of God genuine forgiveness can still be freely given so we, like Joseph, learn to trust the active presence of God in our own lives and believe its possibilities in theirs.

Lundeen affirms this, "Forgiveness opens space for a personal God who takes free, restoring initiatives. God as the ground and goal of all human endeavor is not some rigid reality that we simply bump up against. God is not a kind of impersonal lawmaker or an objective judge who stands at a distance from human affairs. Stressing forgiveness makes God, as ultimate context, a personal and caring reality in whom human life has place and meaning . . . If the dynamics of forgiveness on a human level prompts us to look to God, the whole history of God in Christ presses toward center stage. In Christ forgiveness is made clear. The deep personal dimensions of freedom in relationships sur-

face. God is seen as the lover who suffers for the guilty in
such a dependable and decisive way that we can build all
our hope around him."[6]

With this affirmation pointing us to Jesus Christ, let us
find a second biblical example of the importance of forgiveness in the words of our Savior himself:

> Luke 17:1–10
> Jesus said to his disciples: "Things that cause people to
> sin are bound to come, but woe to that person through whom
> they come. It would be better for him to be thrown into the
> sea with a millstone tied around his neck than for him to
> cause one of these little ones to sin. So watch yourselves. If
> your brother sins, rebuke him, and if he repents, forgive him.
> If he sins against you seven times in a day, and seven times
> comes back to you and says, 'I repent,' forgive him." The
> apostles said to the Lord, "Increase our faith!" He replied,
> "If you have faith as small as a mustard seed, you can say to
> this mulberry tree, 'Be uprooted and planted in the sea,' and
> it will obey you. Suppose one of you had a servant plowing
> or looking after the sheep. Would he say to the servant when
> he comes in from the field, 'Come along now and sit down
> to eat?' Would he not rather say, 'Prepare my supper, get
> yourself ready and wait on me while I eat and drink; after
> that you may eat and drink'? Would he thank the servant be-
> cause he did what he was told to do? So you also, when you
> have done everything you were told to do, should say, 'We
> are unworthy servants; we have only done our duty.'"

Jesus begins his remarks to his disciples with the realism we have come to expect from our incarnate Lord; realism about the frequency and seriousness of sin; about our
own susceptibility and the step-by-patient-step nature of
forgiveness.

The glory of the miracle that is forgiveness blazes forth
against the darkly somber picture Jesus gives his disciples
of the stern judgment due to those who cause others to sin.
Better to die a violent death than to be responsible for the

temptation of a vulnerable brother or sister (vv. 1–3a)! In light of this fearful condemnation of the kind of betrayal of trusting human relationships of which we all are capable, how welcome and wondrous is the possibility of forgiveness!

The hard work that is forgiveness is the next topic of Jesus' teaching: Forgiveness is a process involving repeated condescension to the failures of the one who has offended you. ("Seven times a day" means there is no end to the responsibility to forgive. Compare Jesus' expansion on this principle in Matthew 18:21–22, "seventy times seven".) The disciples are overwhelmed by the difficulty of such a standard of behavior. How much faith are we going to need to be *that* forgiving? To take risks with people like *that*? To be *that* vulnerable to further hurt? Jesus' reply to their astonished query is that it isn't really a matter at all of how much more faith they will need; a little faith is potentially powerful beyond ordinary expectations (v. 6)! It is really a matter of obedient effort, growing out of an understanding of our own humanness and the servant-Lord nature of our commitment to God.

Once again, as we saw in Joseph's life, ability to forgive involves my reinterpreting my position as victim: Am I really superior to the culprit who injured me? Are we not more alike than unlike? This recognition does not excuse their action or their responsibility to repent (v. 3, "... rebuke him, and if he repents. . . ."), but it is a vital step toward becoming ready to forgive and it does not involve some esoteric level of spirituality. Forgiveness is not only for the spiritually advanced!

Using a typical day in the life of a household servant, Jesus next tells a parable to illustrate this principle in forgiving someone who has hurt you, even repeatedly. The parable is keenly realistic; the servant's task was against personal feelings and comfort, very hard at the moment and apparently thankless. (Jesus does not condone slavery, but simply uses a slice of life in current society to make his point. On another occasion in Luke 12:35–37, he tells a parable in which the master reverses the normal roles and humbly serves his servants. That story symbolizes God's grace to us, this one symbolizes our proper servant attitude toward one another.) The disciples' need in forgiving was not more faith, but to use the faith which they already had and obey God's will that they forgive.

Forgiveness is not initially a feeling; it is chosen actions, by which, even before you can feel forgiving, you carry out forgiveness by not using past (six failures already today!) offenses against the offender. You can at least take beginning steps, even if you have to put it in terms of only doing your duty (v. 10) and finding a way to begin the work of the forgiveness process.

Both of these scriptural examples clearly present the crucial importance of forgiveness. For Joseph it meant being released from bondage to the past by forgiving the almost unforgivable cruelties of his brothers. For Jesus' disciples it meant that the peril of condemnation for sin in relationships is matched by the miracle of forgiving grace. That miracle is one which can be repeated in our own choices toward those who sin against us.

The power of forgiveness is incalculable, its place in healing emotional wounds is crucial, and it is a miracle repeated beyond the pages of Scripture in the lives of God's people today. Forgiveness is important because it is the only solution to the hurts and brokenness we experience both as people who sin and are sinned against. Forgiveness offers us a fresh start. It is the good news that is at the core of Christianity.

2

The Possibility
of Forgiveness

The possibility of forgiveness is rooted in the character and actions of God. If we lived in a universe created and governed by anyone other than the Christian God, there would be no hope of forgiveness. The forgiveness of our own sins as well as our forgiveness of the sins of others against us and our forgiveness of ourselves for our own sins are all made possible by who God is and what he has done.

As with the other graces of the Christian life, the origin of forgiveness lies first and foremost in the character of God himself. This, then, must be our starting point in considering the possibility of our giving and receiving forgiveness.

God's Forgiveness Is Rooted in His Eternal Character

In the midst of the worst crisis of his troubled leadership of Israel, the judgment of the people for their worship of the golden calf, Moses, fearful of losing God's presence, prays to see God's glory (Exod. 32–34). In response, God reveals himself by proclaiming his name, "the LORD," and the moral character that name encompasses.

> Then the LORD came down in the cloud and stood there with him and proclaimed his name, the LORD. And he passed in front of Moses, proclaiming, "The LORD, the LORD, the compassionate and gracious God, slow to anger, abounding in love and faithfulness, maintaining love to thousands, and forgiving wickedness, rebellion and sin. Yet he does not leave the guilty unpunished. . . . " (Exodus 34:5–7)

In this disclosure, echoed in later Scriptures (e.g., Neh. 9:17; Ps. 86:15; Joel 2:13), God shows that forgiveness is foundational to his nature. As we shall consider later, he also shows that forgiveness is not incompatible with realism about the guilt of human sin.

When did God begin to be a forgiving God? At the cross? In the exodus? When he pronounced judgment upon Satan with the first promise of a Savior for fallen humankind? (Gen. 3:15). Scripture compels us to deduce that forgiveness is part of God's *eternal* character! It was God's nature before it was needed!

- "This grace was given us in Christ Jesus before the beginning of time . . . ." (2 Tim. 1:9).
- "He chose us in him before the creation of the world to be holy and blameless in his sight" (Eph. 1:4).

If the incomparable and timeless mystery of God's eternal plan for our salvation existed before sin, then the heart of God was a forgiving heart before human hearts chose evil! We cannot explain it, but like the apostles who put this truth into the context of thanksgiving (1 Thess. 1:4–6; 2:13; 1 Peter 1:20–21), we can only praise the God who is the source of such blessing.

God's Forgiveness Is Incomparable

The hope of our ever being able to forgive others is grounded in the incomparably wondrous nature of God's own forgiveness. Our hope lies in the fact that God's forgiveness is immeasurably superior to ours. This should not be cause for despair but for rejoicing.

> God's forgiveness cannot be understood by analyzing the nature of human forgiveness. When Israel was invited to salvation in the way of repentance, the promise of comfort was added that God would have mercy and abundantly pardon (Isa. 55:6–7). But it was also stated that "'My thoughts are not your thoughts, neither are your ways my ways,' declares the LORD. 'As the heavens are higher than the earth, so are my ways higher than your ways and my thoughts than your thoughts'" (55:8–9). Therefore, the divine forgiveness could only be heard and accepted as the content of a truly new and astonishing *tidings of salvation*. . . . God, we read, shall "tread our iniquities under foot" and "cast all our sins into the depths of the sea" (Micah 7:19); he shall sweep them away as a cloud and mist (Isa. 44:22) and cast them behind his back (38:17). In all of this, as Israel's God, he cannot be *compared*. "Who is a God like thee, pardoning iniquity . . . ?"[1]

In this fact there should be great comfort for us because God's forgiveness is presented to us in the Bible as incomparably available and enduring. What hope we are given that our sins can never exhaust God's mercy!

But help in making forgiveness possible comes to us from God in the form of yet another truth about his nature.

God's Forgiveness Is Coupled with His Realism About Sin

We must not construe from God's forgiving nature that he is, therefore, indifferent to sin. When, for example, in the process of dealing with our emotional wounds we undertake to reexperience the pain suffered at the hands of another person, we need to understand that we have God's example when we refuse to ignore the reality of the wrong done to us. God's forgiveness of sin is certainly not an overlooking of the gravity of the offense. God does not easily forgive because he was never really angry. Our anger at those who hurt us is at least in this way like God's anger—it is real. God never avoids the true nature of our evil human behavior.

- ". . . forgiving wickedness, rebellion and sin. Yet he does not leave the guilty unpunished. . . ." (Exod. 34:7).
- "Woe to those who call evil good and good evil, who put darkness for light and light for darkness, who put bitter for sweet and sweet for bitter" (Isa. 5:20).
- "If we claim to be without sin, we deceive ourselves and the truth is not in us. If we confess our sins, he is faithful and just and will forgive us our sins and purify us from all unrighteousness. If we claim we have not sinned, we make him out to be a liar and his word has no place in our lives" (1 John 1:8–10).

One of the clearest truths in the biblical message is that God's forgiveness is not set in the context of watering down or relativizing human sin. To the contrary, God is revealed to be truly and consistently angry with sin.

"Divine forgiveness is never, in Scripture, an indifferent love or a matter of God's *being blind*. It is rather a turning from real *wrath* to real *grace* . . . the Bible's message (is) of jubilee and forgiveness—a message tied together in a single package with the knowledge of the wrath of God against man's sin."[2]

This realistic anger of God against evil is consistently seen in the life and ministry of Jesus. Significantly it is Jesus, the "Lamb of God who takes away the sin of the world" (John 1:29), who is "led like a lamb to the slaughter" with the "iniquity of us all" upon his innocent soul. It is this same Jesus who suffers for us in silent submission (Isa. 53:6–7), but who is said to be unswervingly wrathful with sin. In judgment the wicked cry out to be hidden from "the face of him who sits on the throne and from the *wrath of the Lamb*"!

So we find that God's forgiveness is a miracle, accomplished without overlooking the reality and destructiveness of human sin for a moment. It is against the dark backdrop of real evil that God reveals his grace in its impact on the guilty human heart.

- "For his anger lasts only a moment, but his favor lasts a lifetime. Weeping may remain for a night, but rejoicing comes in the morning" (Ps. 30:5).
- "I will heal their waywardness and love them freely, for my anger has turned away from them" (Hos. 14:4).

This brings us to another unique factor in the forgiveness that comes from the Lord himself.

God's Forgiveness Is Embraced in His Justice

We know that the key question of the New Testament, indeed of the whole Bible, is "How can God be just and yet be the justifier of sinners?" How can God be truly angry at sin, truly punish sin, yet truly forgive a sinner and continue to be holy and just?

Here the gospel points to the cross as the focus of God's justice. It is precisely there, where the Son of God suffers the anger of God in our place, that the gospel shows us how seriously God takes sin and how justly he accomplishes forgiving grace. Sin *is* paid for; sin *is* justly punished. At the cross God's mercy and grace cut through the problem of just punishment for our sins. But it is not fair! It is not fair for Jesus to suffer for the guilty—for my guilt! No, it is not, but here, here in this Great Unfairness lies the power that not only makes it possible for God to forgive me, but also for me to learn to forgive those who hurt me! What we learn from God's forgiveness of us is that forgiveness doesn't have anything to do with fairness. Forgiveness cuts through the whole question of just deserts.

The heart of the possibility of forgiveness is that God forgives because his justice has been satisfied, satisfied by the atonement provided by his love in giving his only Son for us. As "unfair" as that solution is, it is an unfairness absorbed into the heart of God by his merciful acceptance of the unfairness!

The Doctrine of Divine Satisfaction

But let us look more carefully at this biblical word "satisfied." What we shall see is that it carries a richness of understanding which can begin to unlock our own power to forgive.

The doctrine of divine satisfaction is the biblical teaching that Christ, by offering his sinless life in our place, bore the full, rightful punishment for our sin, suffering all that the law of God required of sinners and, therefore, satisfied God's justice forever and set us free from all obligation to atone for our own sins. The atonement is rooted in both the love and justice of God. Love offered sinners a way of escape while justice demanded that the requirements of the law should be met (John 3:16; Rom. 3:24–26). The atonement served, therefore, to render satisfaction to God because his Son bore the penalty of sin and met the demands of the law.

What has this doctrine to do with our ability to forgive those who hurt us? Just this: By the power of the Holy Spirit we may share in God's satisfaction even if we receive little or no satisfaction within our human relationship with the one who hurt us. This is the great psychological implication of the theology of divine satisfaction.

When I have been wronged, I may feel I can only forgive if certain requirements are met. For example, I may judge that I can only be satisfied if the wrong is acknowledged, the wrong is punished, and that which was wrongly taken from me can be restored. Let us consider each of these in turn.

1. *I may feel that the wrong must be acknowledged.* In the best scenario, the one who sinned against me will come to see the wrong and confess it to me. But suppose he or she does not acknowledge that wrong was done?

While the one who hurt me may not acknowledge the wrong, God my Heavenly Father does. Thus, the only one who can fully and accurately assess the nature of the crime, agrees with me that I have indeed been wronged. The only one (God) able to realize the true depth of my pain faces the realities of that suffering with me (Isa. 63:9, "In all their distress he too was distressed . . ."). Can I be satisfied with that?

2. *I may feel that the wrong must be punished.* In the best of situations, guilty persons are convicted and pay the appropriate penalty for their offenses. But suppose the one who has hurt me is never brought to task for their deeds done to me? The culprit may not be punished, but Christ my Savior was. Just as he died for the sins I have committed, so he also died for the sins committed against me. Justice is done in the highest court! I think I would be satisfied if my tormentor, a finite creature, was made to pay the price for the wrong done to me. But the price actually paid was so much more costly, even the infinite life of the Son of God! Can I be satisfied with that?

3. *I may feel that what was wrongly taken from me must be restored.* But it rarely can be. Not often can the culprit give back what he or she has "stolen." A childhood spoiled by abuse, marriage broken by unfaithfulness, friendship shattered by betrayal; too much is lost that cannot be replaced— it is lost in irretrievable time. The perpetrator may not be willing or able to compensate for what cannot be undone.

But God promises to do so! Ultimately in heaven, and partly now in the healing fellowship of the Body of Christ, God will restore all that is lost.

God satisfied his Son for his suffering ("After the suffering of his soul, he will see the light of life, and be satisfied. . . ." Isa. 53:11) and God will satisfy us for ours. ("And I, in righteousness, I will see your face; when I awake, I will be satisfied with seeing your likeness," Ps. 17:15.)

Can I now be satisfied with God's promise of satisfaction? Can I live without compensation from those who hurt me and can I, through trust in God, find grace to forgive the culprit? All these things are possible because of what God has done and who he is.

How can I rise to this level of being satisfied, of letting God's satisfaction be mine? The Father is satisfied with the sacrifice of the Son; the Son is satisfied by the resurrection and exaltation given him by the Father; now the Scripture seems to indicate that the Holy Spirit can impact the results of that divine satisfaction to me. The satisfied mind of Christ is given to us and we are instructed that we can experience the attitudes of his mind ("We have the mind of Christ," 1 Cor. 2:16; "Your attitude should be the same as that of Christ Jesus," Phil. 2:5).

This mind is created in you with the new life impacted by the Spirit when he brings you out of death into life; when he makes you begin to be a new creation (2 Cor. 5:17); when he begins the "renewing of your mind" that transforms your thinking (Rom. 12:2) about life's choices and the people in your world.

> We cannot sacrifice enough to heal the one who hurts us. We are not able to forgive equal to our spouse's sinning—nor when such giving must come solely from ourselves. But if forgiveness is a tool, it is also a power tool whose power comes from a source other than ourselves. We may use it; we may carefully and self-consciously apply it to our spouses; but Jesus Christ empowers it. He is the true source of its transfiguring love. And the love of the Son of God is infinite.[3]

Walter Wangerin Jr. makes this statement out of his own experience of being forgiven by his wife, Thanne, for long offending her tender spirit. His description of their experience illustrates well how the mind that shares this satisfaction of God can be enabled to forgive beyond human possibility:

> Thanne could not forgive me. This is a plain fact. My sin was greater than her capacity to forgive, had lasted longer than her kindness, had grown more oppressive than her goodness. This was not a single act nor a series of acts, but my being. My sin was the murder of her spirit, the unholy violation of her sole identity—the blithe assumption of her presence, as though she were furniture. I had broken her. How could a broken person be at the same time whole enough to forgive? No: Thanne was created finite, and could not forgive me.
>
> But Jesus could.
>
> One day Thanne stood in the doorway of my study, looking at me. I turned in my chair and saw that she was not angry. Small Thanne, delicate, diminutive Thanne, she was not glaring, but gazing at me with gentle, questioning eyes. This was totally unexpected, both her presence and her expression. There was no reason why she should be standing there, no detail I've forgotten to tell you. Yet, for a full minute we looked at one another; and then she walked to my side where I sat. She touched my shoulder. She said, "Wally, will you hug me?" I leaped from my chair, I wrapped her all around in two arms and squeezed my wife, my wife, so deeply in my body—and we both burst into tears.
>
> Would I hug her? Oh, but the better question was, would she let me hug her? And she did. Dear Lord Jesus, where did this come from, this sudden, unnatural, undeserved willingness to let me touch her, hug her, love her? Not from me! I was her ruination. Not from her, because I had killed that part of her. From you!
>
> How often had we hugged before? I couldn't count the times. How good had those hugs been? I couldn't measure the goodness. But *this* hug—don't you know, it was my salvation, different from any other and more remarkable be-

cause this is the hug I should never have had. *That* is forgiveness! The law was gone. Rights were all abandoned.
Mercy took their place. We were married again. And it was
you, Christ Jesus, in my arms—within my graceful Thanne.
One single, common hug, and we were alive again.

Thanne gave me a gift: She gave me the small plastic figure of a woman with her eyes rolled up, her mouth skewed
to one side, the tongue lolling out, a cartoon face. I have this
gift in my study today.

The inscription at the bottom reads: "I love you so much
it hurts."[4]

Indeed, the work of forgiving love can hurt. But leaving
satisfaction to God paradoxically opens us up to the possibility of experiencing the benefits of forgiveness. For the
Wangerins, the beginning of their experience of the miracle of forgiveness was allowing the mind of Christ to be created in them. The truth is that because of who God is and
what he has done, I do not need to have the wrong acknowledged to me, I do not need to arrange for the punishment of the offender, and I do not need to demand that
they restore to me what they took from me. God, our Father, will see to each of these things. This is the foundation
of my giving forgiveness and is the start of my movement
toward freedom.

3

The Necessity
of Forgiveness

A strange story entitled "Cold Storage" was published by neurologist Dr. Oliver Sacks in the British quarterly *Granta*, and reported in the *New Yorker Magazine*.[1] In it Dr. Sacks described a patient, identified as Uncle Toby, whom he met in 1957 in London. While making a house call to see a sick child, another doctor saw Uncle Toby sitting silent and motionless in a corner of a room. When he asked about the figure, the family explained matter-of-factly, "That's Uncle Toby. He's hardly moved in seven years."

Uncle Toby's initial slowing down had been so gradual as to go almost unnoticed. Later, it became so profound that it was just accepted by the family. "He was fed and watered daily," Dr. Sacks reports. "He was really no trouble . . . Most people never noticed him, still, silent in the corner. He was not regarded as ill; he had just come to a stop." Uncle Toby, it turned out, was suffering from a thyroid malfunction, and his metabolic rate had been reduced to almost zero. His temperature, which had to be measured on a special thermometer, proved to be sixty-eight degrees Fahrenheit—thirty degrees below normal. He was, in Dr. Sacks' words, "alive, but not alive; in abeyance, in cold storage." Over a period of weeks, doctors administered progressively larger doses of thyroxine to Uncle Toby, and his temperature rose steadily; soon he was walking and talking. Within a month, Dr. Sacks says, Uncle Toby had "awakened."

Most of the rest of the case study details the remarkable situations of both Uncle Toby, for whom not a moment had passed during the previous seven years, and his doctors, who were trying to decide how they might best coax their patient toward a realization of his predicament. But then the case took a darkly ironic turn. The doctors discovered that Uncle Toby had a highly malignant, rapidly proliferating "oat-cell" carcinoma. They managed to find x-rays taken seven years earlier and discovered early signs, overlooked at the time, of the cancer he now had. Such cancers ordinarily kill within a few months, but "it seemed that his cancer, like the rest of him, had been arrested, in cold storage," Dr. Sacks writes. Once he was warmed up, the growth of cancer increased rapidly and he expired several days later.[2]

There is an emotional and spiritual principle illustrated by this story, for guilt unforgiven or anger unreleased by forgiving can ultimately only damage us. We can deny, repress, and put our anger into "cold storage," but it will only come to life again sometime in the future! Body, mind, and spirit are inevitably, even if slowly, poisoned by unforgiven sin or by anger and resentment. The Bible bears solemn witness to this. Consider, for example, David, who tried to avoid dealing with his guilt and tells us:

> When I kept silent, my bones wasted away through my
> groaning all day long. For day and night your hand was
> heavy upon me; my strength was sapped as in the heat of
> summer. Then I acknowledged my sin to you . . . and you
> forgave the guilt of my sin. (Psalm 32:3–5)

Experience affirms the Bible's witness and finds the
bondage of the angry to be no less harmful than that of
the guilty. Author Dennis Guernsey writes, "I have really
hated only one person in my life. I mean hatred that is ob-
sessive. Hatred you can't let go of. The experience of hatred is still vivid in my memory. What I remember most
is the addictive nature of the hatred. I got to where I liked
thinking about my feelings toward the person. I fanta-
sized about what I wished would happen to him. The
thoughts about the situation that provoked my hatred
would not go away. I soon came to realize that the hatred
was controlling me rather than me controlling it. I was
hooked."[3]

We harbor grudges, often against ourselves, and the
stress of that unresolved anger may well result in physical
illness, as well as unhealed, wounded relationships. "Try a
simple experiment on yourself. Make a fist and hold it tight.
One minute of this is sufficient to bring discomfort. Consider what would happen if the fist were maintained in that
state of tension during a period that extended into weeks,
months, or even years. Obviously it would soon become a
sick member of the body."[4]

You may hurt a person by not forgiving them and thus
feel some satisfying sense of getting even, but almost without exception, the hurt you do to yourself may be even
greater. You may not after awhile feel the pain of the
clenched resentment in your soul, but its self-inflicted paral-
ysis will have its effect upon your whole life.

Understanding the way in which unresolved anger can
paralyze and destroy us from within requires that we understand the role of anger in emotional wounds.

The Psychology of Emotional Wounds

The first response to the experience of emotional hurt is a sense of loss. It is common for this loss to be covered by anger so quickly that most people are unaware that it is a part of their response to hurt. Emotional wounds always leave us with some diminished sense of self. It may be a loss of self-esteem or possibly of our sense of self-competence or worth. I experience the violations of trust usually involved in being wounded by another as something having been taken away from me. Indeed the common, often tearful cry of the victim of some form of abuse is, "I find it almost impossible now to really trust anyone!"

The dominant feelings associated with this experience of loss are those of vulnerability and sadness. But another feeling that often accompanies hurt is a feeling of being alone, of being abandoned or isolated. These feelings give particularly clear evidence of how central loss is to the experience of hurt. The pain associated with the experience of abandonment by a loved one, particularly a person on whom one depends for one's very existence, is probably as intense as emotional pain gets. But even when the feeling of abandonment is not part of the experience of hurt, the sense of loss is. Failure to begin to follow the way of forgiveness will inevitably only increase this sense of loss in the unforgiving person.

The feelings of anger usually come quickly after being the victim of hurt. Anger may be a very constructive force when it mobilizes us to action in response to some injustice or evil. However, anger may also fail us by being only a distraction for our pain and turning into a preoccupation with retaliatory fantasies, or when it moves us to inappropriate expression, which hurts others, or to repression, which hurts us. Further, the expression of anger is often very subtle. It can appear in many different guises, each of which masks to some extent the actual core of anger: depression, suspicion, jealousy, impatience, cynicism, and passive-aggressive

behavior. With one or more of these faces, anger shows itself to be a part of the experience of hurt and an ongoing
consequence of refusal to begin the process of forgiving.[5]

Unresolved and unrealized anger has a capacity to damage body and soul in ways that are unequaled by any other
emotion. But what about its effects on one's spiritual life?
Few warnings in Scripture are worded more strongly than
those that confront our refusal or reluctance to forgive.

> For if you forgive men when they sin against you, your heav-
> enly Father will also forgive you. But if you do not forgive
> men their sins, your Father will not forgive your sins.
> (Matthew 6:14–15)

> "'You wicked servant,'" he said, "I canceled all that debt of
> yours because you begged me to. Shouldn't you have had
> mercy on your fellow servant just as I had on you?"
> (Matthew 18:32–33)

But even more powerful than these warnings should be
the appeal to our hearts to remember how deeply we have
been forgiven and how costly was the love that accomplished that forgiveness.

> As God's chosen people, holy and dearly loved, clothe your-
> selves with compassion, kindness, humility, gentleness and
> patience. Bear with each other and forgive whatever griev-
> ances you may have against one another. Forgive as the
> Lord forgave you. (Colossians 3:12–13)

Forgiveness is necessary for freedom from the exhausting
attempt to construct and maintain a "balance of payments"
kind of relationship between culprit and victim. This contractual arrangement for exchange of social courtesies, this
peace conference treaty for cessation of hostilities may make
coexistence possible, but it demands constant monitoring for
fairness and creates ongoing anxiety about shifts in the balance of power. Forgiveness cuts through the complicated system of checks and balances by bringing in a miraculously re-

freshing and releasing kind of imbalance. Like God's forgiveness in Christ there is an initiative of grace that liberates, amazes, and wins with the immeasurable power of love.

> Before God, the very meaning of our lives depends upon a power from beyond us that sustains, renews, and preserves. Forgiveness is a way of seeing that power in its most radically supportive role . . . to return to the human scene with a resolve not to absolutize any form of calculation as the ultimate path to wholeness. Rights are important, but they are not enough. No strict accounting will do . . . going beyond fairness is the answer. The forgiving initiative may be ours or another's, but the willingness to 'hang a little loose' in relationships is precisely what forgiveness requires and what forgiveness brings into the picture. It builds community and relationship by letting things be unequal.[6]

Forgiveness is necessary also for honesty in human relationships. Without that honesty the future of a relationship is always in jeopardy. Honesty comes with confession and appeal for forgiveness on the part of the perpetrator, and honesty comes when the forgiver takes the strides in reinterpreting hurt that introduces new truth into the situation. Until that point our damaged emotions tend to distort how we perceive both the one who hurt us and ourselves. In our woundedness, our perceptions are shaped by our feelings. For healing to occur, our perceptions must be brought into line with reality, with truth. The essence of this reinterpretation of our hurt is seeing those who hurt us as separate from what they did to us and seeing ourselves as more than our wound.

The power of forgiveness is included in the power of the truth that sets us free (John 8:32). Forgiveness is necessary for freedom from the irreversible past. Sometimes our pain comes from the memory of hurt at the hands of those beyond our reach: the person who betrayed us and will never acknowledge it; the "monster" whose ruthless actions destroyed many lives and left countless others scarred; the abusive parent or sibling who died unrepentant and unforgiven. Such persons retain power over our lives if we allow the haunting memories to control us. They have no opportunity to repay us good for the evil they did, even if they could now admit and regret their actions, and our memories cannot be erased. Is there enough miracle in the hard work of forgiveness to bring some peace to our hearts when there can be no redress of our grievances, no access to a hard heart barred against us forever?

The Bible gives us hope for such, telling us that bitter roots do not need to "grow up to cause trouble" (Heb. 12:15) and that at the "throne of grace" there is one who understands hurt and has grace for help in any need (Heb. 4:14–15), which must include even the grace of forgiving. Moreover, there is for us in the gospel such a promise of inclusion in family that our continuing pain from irreversible rejection can begin to fade as we learn more of that familial embrace by our Father and his other children. The Spirit will "testify with our spirit that we are God's children . . . heirs of God and co-heirs with Christ . . ." (Rom. 8:16–17). Such rich love makes it possible to live with the unfairness of unsettled emotional accounts.

The crucial necessities of forgiveness are seen in that most intriguing of stories, the parable of the prodigal son. A particularly helpful perspective on forgiveness is found if we enter the story through the mind of the older brother.

There was a man who had two sons. The younger one said to his father, "Father, give me my share of the estate." So he divided his property between them. Not long after that, the younger son got together all he had, set off for a distant country and there squandered his wealth in wild living. After he had spent everything, there was a severe famine in that whole country, and he began to be in need. So he went and hired himself out to a citizen of that country, who sent him to his field to feed pigs. He longed to fill his stomach with the pods that the pigs were eating, but no one gave him anything. When he came to his senses, he said, "How many of my father's hired men have food to spare, and here I am starving to death!

I will set out and go back to my father and say to him: Father,
I have sinned, against heaven and against you. I am no longer
worthy to be called your son; make me like one of your hired
men." So he got up and went to his father. But while he was
still a long way off, his father saw him and was filled with
compassion for him; he ran to his son, threw his arms around
him and kissed him. The son said to him, "Father, I have
sinned against heaven and against you. I am no longer worthy to be called your son." But the father said to his servants,
"Quick! Bring the best robe and put it on him. Put a ring on
his finger and sandals on his feet. Bring the fattened calf and
kill it. Let's have a feast and celebrate. For this son of mine
was dead and is alive again; he was lost and is found." So they
began to celebrate. Meanwhile, the older son was in the field.
When he came near the house, he heard music and dancing.
So he called one of the servants and asked him what was
going on. "Your brother has come," he replied, "and your father has killed the fattened calf because he has him back safe
and sound." The older brother became angry and refused to
go in. So his father went out and pleaded with him. But he
answered his father, "Look! All these years I've been slaving
for you and never disobeyed your orders. Yet you never gave
me even a young goat so I could celebrate with my friends.
But when this son of yours who has squandered your property with prostitutes comes home, you kill the fattened calf
for him!" "My son," the father said, "you are always with me,
and everything I have is yours. But we had to celebrate and
be glad, because this brother of yours was dead and is alive
again; he was lost and is found." (Luke 15:11–32)

We can use the older brother to clobber ourselves with
guilt: If we cannot forgive someone we are just like this
proud, angry, holier-than-thou, wretched brother standing
outside in the dark, hurting the heart of his loving father! Or
we can heap scorn on the older brother, perhaps because we
know Jesus is telling the story to the Pharisees and we choose
to identify the older brother—not ourselves—with them.

But let us not miss the tone of the parable. Jesus is much
more gentle toward this character in his story than we usu-

ally are. He uses the older brother to speak a lovingly urgent appeal to the Pharisees to join his celebration of the salvation of the lost. The older brother is not a bad guy, he is the hardworking son of his father who has been hurt, has seen his father hurt, and needs, like each of us, to learn how to forgive and be reconciled to those who have hurt us.

The parable is an incomplete story. Jesus may have wanted to creatively stimulate our imagination and have us write the ending in our own minds. Suppose the older brother were to be reconciled to his younger brother. What hard work would be necessary to be part of the miracle of forgiveness?

First, he would have to recognize a foundation for their relationship. If he would listen to his father's poignant appeal he would be reminded of that foundation: "My son . . . this brother of yours . . ." (vv. 31–32). The father echoes and calls back for reconsideration his older son's bitter allusion to "this son of yours who has squandered your property" (v. 30). The father is trying to say, "You are *both* my children!" There is the foundation for a reconciliation; they both need the love and forgiveness of the same father.

Second, to be reconciled to his brother, the older of the sons would need to ask the father's help to see his brother with new eyes. If he was not yet able to trust his brother or the motives that brought him home, at least he would need to see his brother in the present not just through eyes of the past: "This brother of yours was dead and is alive again; he was lost and is found" (v. 32). The older brother is saying to his father: "How dare he come back! Don't you see the injustice?" The father is saying to his son: "He's back! He's back! Don't you see the miracle?" *Again, to move toward reconciliation the older brother would have to accept and begin small steps in forgiveness.* "The older brother became angry and refused to go in. So his father went out and pleaded with him" (v. 28).

The father must dearly have wanted his sons reconciled completely, but all that seems to be the issue at the moment, that is until the older brother widened the issue, was would he join the party? He could be angry still, but would he just let the distance between him and his brother decrease for a while? Would he try a first step?

In the pilgrimage of forgiveness we need to start where we are, not where we would be if we had some imagined greater strength of will, but where we are now.

Writing of the process of his reconciliation with a friend after a painful and confusing estrangement, Dr. Lewis Smedes remembers: "Forgiveness did come. It came by fits and starts, trickles, driblets of it seeping down the drains of our mutual resentments, but it did come . . . with an unexpected meeting here, a gesture there, the exchange of a greeting, and a hint that better feelings were beginning to flow. We floundered into forgiving. . . . Not a triumph of forgiver's art, I agree. But healing often comes on the wings of trivia . . . Ordinary people forgive best if they go at it in bits and pieces, and for specific acts. . . . forgiving anything at all is a minor miracle; forgiving carte blanche is silly. Nobody can do it. Except God."[7]

Jesus may want us to ask ourselves this about the story of the prodigal: What might have happened if the older brother had at least gone with his father into the house, for even a few minutes?

Third, to be reconciled to his brother, the older son would have to accept the scars caused by his brother's selfish desertion of the family. By this we mean, first of all, that he must absorb the loss caused by his brother's action. The brother is justly and appropriately angry. His younger brother had betrayed their father's kindness and left him to pick up the pieces: "All these years I've been slaving. . . ." (v. 29). The father, in turn, acknowledges the unfairness of the situation, saying: "My son, you are always with me. . . . " (v. 31), thus assuring his son, "I know, you too have been wronged, we're not ignoring that. I know this is hard for you."

There is no argument that the son's anger is excessive. The argument is, though, that his anger can now begin to give way to something more satisfying, a new future of peace, if he will learn to leave "loose ends dangling," "the scales off balance"; and "to accept a score that neither of them can make come out even." Accepting the scars also means learning to trust his father with what it costs to forgive. He will need to hear the power and promise in his father's words: "Everything I have is yours" (v. 31). He must not fear the future; he won't really lose by forgiving, though it may seem so now. The father is saying, as our Father says to us, "Trust the same generosity in me for you that you see me give to your brother."

Related to this is the fact that the guarantee for the future comes only from the father. There is no information in the parable to tell us what the returning brother may be able to give of himself to his older sibling. He has come home to the *father*; that's all we know (v. 18). The younger may be capable of doing very little to improve his relationship with the older.

But the older brother still needs to trust his father, absorb his losses, and forgive his brother because he needs to forgive for his father's sake—and for his own sake. We already know the dangers to the health of body and soul that come from the refusal to forgive, but there is another reason woven into this marvelous parable, a reason why forgiveness is for our own sake: We ought not to miss the celebration!

As originally told by Jesus, the context of this story was the muttering of his disciples that Jesus welcomed sinners. Seeing their grim mood, he told this and two other stories, each revolving around a gathering for joyful celebration (Luke 15:5–9, 23). When we forgive someone who hurt us, we join the rejoicing heart of God, we share his contagious pleasure in showing mercy, we reflect the love that gave us our own pardon and received us back from our own rebellion. It is no accident that Jesus told these stories featuring the joy of restoration. He wants us where he is, at the welcome home feast!

The Feelings of the Unforgiven

Unforgiven guilt manifests itself in a gamut of unpleasant feelings. These fall into three general groupings: fear of punishment or a self-inflicted punishment; loss of self-esteem; loneliness, rejection, or isolation. S. Bruce Narramore summarizes some of the answers given when people are asked how they felt when they felt guilty. Here are some of their replies:

> Scared, uneasy. Tense, like maybe I'm going to get caught. A feeling of impending punishment. Like if somebody finds out I'll be punished and they will scream what I've done to everyone. My mind has a tendency to kick itself several times. Disgusted with myself. Like a raunchy person or a complete failure. Stupid, low, remorseful. Miserable and ashamed. Rotten inside, worthless. A feeling of separation. Lonely and very frustrated. I feel nobody loves me—especially God. I find it hard to like myself. Depressed and separated from others.[8]

It seems that many of the same feelings experienced by the victim of wrongs are also the experience of the remorseful perpetrator who has not yet come to accept forgiveness: loneliness, anxiety, depression, eating disorders, sexual dysfunction, anger, self-hatred; these and more are the feelings of the unforgiven. The Scripture would see these feelings in a Christian as being part of "the spirit of bondage" dominating the one who does not understand the power of grace or believe that forgiving grace is available in their case.

> For you did not receive a spirit that makes you a slave again to fear, but you received the Spirit of sonship. And by him we cry, "Abba, Father." The Spirit himself testifies with our spirit that we are God's children. Now if we are children, then we are heirs—heirs of God and coheirs with Christ. . . . (Rom. 8:15–17a)

Forgiveness is the answer to feelings of guilt and anger. A refusal to forgive is to nourish these ravenously destructive feelings. Forgiveness is not easy. It is, however, both possible and necessary if we are to be whole.

4

The Difficulty
of Forgiveness

It would be quite hard to forgive a man who is "surly and mean in his dealings"; a man who is "such a wicked man that no one can talk to him." David found it hard to forgive the man described this way in 1 Samuel 25. This rich man, Nabal, had been treated with kindness by David, whose soldiers had protected Nabal's herdsmen from raiding parties. Nabal, in turn, refused to give aid to David and his hungry men during their exile in the desert and had slandered and insulted them. David determined to have revenge and is making his way to the desired slaughter when he is met by Nabal's wife. Abigail intercedes, pleading for David to forgive (v. 28), to trust God's care and grace ("bound securely in the bundle of the living by the Lord your God," v. 29), to trust his cause to God (v. 30), and to seek the lifelong blessing of a conscience free from vengeful bloodshed (v. 31).

Though David relents, accepts her plea, and abandons his plans for revenge, he has anger left over and he cannot help being glad when ten days later Nabal is dead by the hand of God ("Praise be to the Lord, who has upheld my cause against Nabal for treating me with contempt," v. 39).

We, New Testament believers, may look back at David through the cross of Jesus Christ and wonder why David, as a believer in the same God, could not forgive Nabal more completely, as Jesus forgave his enemies. We look back at David through the window of the writings of the apostles and want him to display more patience, kindness, and love—more fruit of the Spirit. We need to remember David's place in the unfolding of salvation history. In God's patient preparation of his people for the ultimate gospel, David's rugged mercy to Nabal surely qualifies as an act of "far-enough-for-the-light-he-had" forgiveness.

Perhaps the story of David, Nabal, and Abigail is better seen as being about not taking vengeance than of forgiveness. At a minimum, David did not act on his vengeful, vindictive feelings. Indeed he did much more, for he turned from vengeful rage to committing his cause to the promises of God for his future, based upon his recognition of God's faithfulness in his past. This much is an equivalent in David to the spirit of new covenant forgiveness: Abigail, in effect, said to David, "Just as God has been good to you, so you be good to us" (vv. 28–29); and we are told to forgive "just as in Christ God forgave" (Eph. 4:32).

We may struggle with anger as did David and for us, too, just not yielding to our vindictive desires may be a long, early, and real step in the pilgrimage of forgiveness. Whatever else we may see in this story, we do see an example of the fact that forgiveness is difficult!

David also illustrates the difficulties on the other side of life's experience with forgiveness: receiving it. His Psalm 32 begins and ends with rejoicing in God's forgiveness ("Blessed . . . Blessed . . . Rejoice . . . be glad . . . sing," vv.

1–2, 11), but between the first and the final cries of joy we find David's testimony to the feelings he suffered while he delayed confessing his sin and accepting God's grace ("wasted . . . groaning . . . heavy . . . strength was sapped," vv. 3–4). We also find his admonition to us to avoid his painful experience by receiving "the Lord's unfailing love," (vv. 5–10). David gives us a picture of physical and emotional torment and begs us not to be stubborn in the face of mercy. Although David's difficulty remembered in Psalm 32 may have been primarily that of acknowledging his sin, a comparison with Psalm 51 leads us to believe that he also suffered an in-between period when, having confessed, he was, however, not yet assured of God's complete forgiveness ("Do not cast me from your presence or take your Holy Spirit from me. Restore to me the joy of your salvation," vv. 11–12). There seems to be a note of uncertainty and tentativeness in these words. It is a plea, a hoped for but not yet realized confidence that God will restore him to his favor.

The very conviction of sin that makes confession and the receiving of forgiveness possible may create fear that one has sinned beyond grace. David seems to know that his sin is so heinous that only God can accomplish effective cleansing of his conscience ("wash me, and I will be whiter than snow," v. 7). "The expression is not one used for washing oneself, but one that refers to the washing of clothes by treading them. It suggests not a polite rinse but a thorough scrub, which presupposes that the object of washing is in a thoroughly disheveled state . . . This is how the psalmist feels."[1]

Only God can forgive, but will he? My fears and shame may deafen me to the answer. Receiving forgiveness may be hard!

Why Is Forgiveness So Difficult to Give?

There are a number of reasons why it is so difficult to forgive another person. Some of these are associated with our anger over the hurt done to us, while others come from our fears of the process of forgiveness, its responsibilities and vulnerabilities.

Anger may be a recurring feeling even after one has decided to forgive. "When you are wronged, that wrong becomes an indestructible reality of your life. When you forgive, you heal your hate for the person who created that reality. But you do not change the facts, and you do not undo all of their consequences. The dead stay dead; the wounded are often crippled still. The reality of evil and its damage to human beings is not magically undone and it can still make us very mad. . . A man does not forget that his father abused him as a child. A woman does not forget that her boss lied to her about her future in the company. You do not forget that a person you loved has taken cheap advantage of you and dropped you when the relationship was not paying off. . . . And when you do remember what happened, how can you remember except in anger?"[2]

In our understandable anger we may resist extending forgiveness because of the ambiguities and inequities involved. It seems unfair that forgiveness is a willing relinquishment of certain rights, often hard fought for rights. In forgiveness you choose not to demand your rights of complete redress for the hurt you have suffered.

"Forgiveness is not a neatly balanced relationship. It exalts the one who forgives to such an important place that dependence on that person shapes life differently. It builds community by letting things be unequal and open-ended. . . . This asymmetrical, unequal pattern in forgiveness makes forgiveness troubling, a kind of cheap way out, certainly it is always tempting to make it work the old-fashioned way where everyone earns what they get."[3] Forgiveness seems to place too much of the burden of reconciliation upon the one who suffered the injustice and damage rather than upon the perpetrator.

In my justified anger I may feel that there are wrongs which prevent complete reconciliation. How far must I go? Writing in *The Christian Century*, Richard P. Lord tells of a woman who came to him with questions about how she could forgive a man who murdered her four sons. A few years earlier, a group of young men had gotten high on drugs, broken into her farmhouse home, killed her boys, and shot and left her for dead. Now one of the convicted criminals had written to tell her that he had become a Christian and asked for her forgiveness.

Her questions had to do with whether forgiving this man meant she must have any dealings with him. Lord reports that she was "not open to a future with those who killed her children. She had no relationship with them before the murders and she desires none now. She hopes they create for themselves a positive future, but one that does not include her. Betty Jane is quite ready to affirm that God is merciful and is hopeful that the murderers of her sons will find a genuine relationship with God. But don't ask her to be responsible for their salvation. Don't ask her to go to them and judge their hearts. Let a representative of the church assume that burden."[4] If forgiving meant including them in her life, she felt forgiving would be impossible.

At the opposite end of the spectrum, it may be that the most difficult person to forgive will be one we have loved and trusted much before they hurt and betrayed us. Love does not, in fact, necessarily make forgiveness easy. Love can complicate the process of forgiveness. Leon Morris observes:

> Let us suppose that some passing tramp breaks into your home and steals something you value highly. In due course he is arrested. He denies that he robbed you, but his guilt is clear. He is caught with the goods, let us say. There is no doubt whatever. You would say to yourself, "Perhaps this poor fellow has never had much of a chance in life. I am a

Christian. I have been forgiven much and I ought to forgive."
So you forgive him. It is as easy as that.

But suppose that the person who robbed you and lied to
you was not a passing tramp, whom you have never seen
before and will never see again, but your best friend. Now
the way of forgiveness is harder. And the thing that makes
it harder, the thing that complicates the situation is just the
fact of your love. Your whole being cries out for the restoration of the earlier state of fellowship. With all your heart
you want to forgive. But precisely because you love your
friend so much, the way to the forgiveness you are so ready
to offer is not easy. And if instead of your friend, the one
who robbed you and lied to you was your son, one to whom
you owe the duty of showing the best way in life, as well as
one whom you love with all your heart, then the way of forgiveness may well be very complicated indeed. Love will
make forgiveness certain, but it will not make it easy.[5]

Again my anger may flow to a large extent not from personal resentment or sorrow, but from a true sense of the right-
ness of punishment for those who ruthlessly injure others. I
may be genuinely concerned for the preservation of moral
responsibility in family, business, church, community, and
nation. I may regard punishment as a necessary deterrent to
the culprit repeating his crime with other victims. Should my
forgiveness release the doer of harm upon someone else?

Finally, the negative feelings that accompany my anger
can be invigorating, can make me feel alive. I may not be
ready to give up the sense of power I feel over the person
who hurt me, who may have controlled my life in their abuse
of selfishness. I felt weak and vulnerable; now my anger has
restored a sense of control over my own life and I fear forgiveness will mean giving up too much of my new power.
Also, there is a fresh feeling of moral superiority in my relationship with the person who hurt me, I am shamed no
longer, and I have gained moral high ground that I do not
wish to surrender.[6]

Resolving Difficulties with Forgiveness

How do we resolve these difficulties? To begin with, and as already indicated, do not be surprised by fresh waves of anger. The goal with our anger is to move beyond malice, to abandon opportunities for vindictive striking back. Though you cannot erase the past, you can get beyond being obsessed with it, being driven by it. In the process of forgiveness you will become less and less focused upon the remembered pain. Your anger will, in time, have less enduring emotional energy. As God gives you hope for a future free for new beginnings, you will find yourself gladly less responsive to the memories of old pain.

When you struggle with the inequities of forgiveness, with the heavier burden that rests upon you, the forgiver, remember that this hard work is also a miracle. God has grace for such sacrifices. It is he who made suffering for the sake of another person a powerful part of forgiveness when he took the punishment for our sins upon himself. It is, therefore, possible that we who "live by the Spirit" should be able to "keep in step with the Spirit" (Gal. 5:22-26) as he enables our new choices in life.

The imbalance in relationships, accepted as part of our forgiving journey, will not be a manipulative, obligation-creating way of controlling another person, though we must avoid that temptation. "In contrast, real forgiveness accepts vicarious suffering as an unavoidable by-product of concern and respect for the other person. It is not suffering sought for its own sake or as a means of asserting power. It is suffering that is taken on as the price of a hopeful future. . . . Forgiveness enriches the future with genuinely new possibilities . . . potential for change, for growth, for renewal."[7]

This is grace-enabled gift giving when there may be little reason to feel love or to expect that love will be adequately returned. Walter Wangerin emphasizes the crucial power in this giving of undeserved kindness as he deals with forgiving in marriage: "Only when the spouse has heard his sin, so that he might anticipate, under the law, some retribution, but receives instead the gestures of love—only then can he begin to change and grow in the same humility which his wife has shown him."[8]

When there have been wrongs that seem to have destroyed all possibility for reconciliation, we may have to find our answers in David's experience with Nabal. We may have to do what we can to move on to a future without vengeance, and trust that God, who will be there in our future, will help us to a conscience finally free from hatred. We may have to pray for grace to pray for grace! God can bring us to the place, like the mother of the murdered boys, where we can hope the culprits will seek and receive his forgiveness even though we are not yet up to being the channel of blessing to them ourselves. Perhaps the apostle Paul had such realism in mind when, while commanding that we "not repay anyone evil for evil," added, *"If it is possible, as far as depends on you,* live at peace with everyone" (Rom. 12:17–18).

When the hurt seems overwhelming because it has come from someone you love, perhaps the key to forgiving is to pray and strive for perspective. Must the offense, betrayal that it is, destroy *all* previous bonds of love between you? Complicated though forgiving such a person may be, try to be specific in your memory of their offenses. And add to such a list another roster, the reasons you have loved them in the past. The Holy Spirit, through Paul, suggests the power of such list-making: "Whatever is true, whatever is noble . . . whatever is admirable—if anything is excellent or praiseworthy—think about such things. . . . And the God of peace will be with you" (Phil. 4:8–9). And also remember the spiritual power of covenant-keeping when we turn for help to our God, who has kept his covenant of grace with his people through all their rebellions. Hear him cry to Israel, "When Israel was a child, I loved him. . . . How can I give you up,

Ephraim?" (Hos. 11:1, 8). Because God has such a heart, he can teach us how not to give up those who break our hearts.

A helpful approach to this is reviewed in Rinda G. Rogers' discussion of "Forgiveness and the Healing of the Family." Rogers refers extensively to work by Margaret Cortrones who suggests that forgiveness is an act of relationship and is a multifaceted act or process. She outlines that process in three parts.

First, "turning," that is a turning toward oneself to acknowledge not only one's own role in the family's damaged relationships, but also one's own sense of being damaged or even abandoned by the family.

Second, "facing," that is, facing reciprocal indebtedness. This refers to hearing the other's story, either through the imagination if the person is not available, or through actual listening if contact can be made.

Third, "reclaiming," which is identifying and owning past and present resources in the relationship. It involves the acceptance of one's legacy by acknowledging what one has given and received in the history of the family, the recall of what existed between the participants in the past, including the invisible loyalties that bound the family together for better or worse.[9]

Are there elements in the relationship that have worked for both parties in the past? Can those elements be part of the rebuilding, no matter how slowly and carefully, of the relationship? Perhaps these steps may help in the regaining of perspective and the reawakening of memories of love, shared in the form of bonds, that the offense need not also destroy though it has broken much.

When we feel that punishment must not be neglected, we must remember that we ought not assume that we are the ones to do the punishing by withholding forgiveness. That would bring us perilously close to crossing the line between punishment and revenge. Retribution is God's business, not ours (Rom. 12:17–19). Dan Hamilton writes:

Vengeance in the Bible is described in detail, hoped for, prayed for, promised. And it is left securely and solely in God's hands. He has reserved it for himself. There are reasons for this. James tells us that "the anger of man does not work the righteousness of God" (1:20). When I was young, I helped my father build things in his workshop. I could do some of the work and use some of the tools, but I was reminded, "Keep your hands off the power tools. They are good tools, and useful in my hands to do what I want done, but they are too powerful and dangerous for you to use." Revenge is a spiritual power tool fitted to God's hand alone.[10]

Related to this may be my resistance to abandoning my anger which gives me the feeling of at last being in control. For long I may have felt victimized and helpless; now it feels good and right to find the "tables turned." The answer to this may lie in understanding that what I really need control over is the power of the past to cruelly influence my life. The hurtful memories, not necessarily the repentant perpetrator, is what I now have in my power.

To forgive is not necessarily to extend unconditional trust. Genuine forgiveness means that I no longer hold the hurt over the head of the other person. It does not mean that I must assume that I will never again be hurt by them, nor does it mean that I should never take steps to minimize this possibility.

Additionally, I must realize that the perceived value, from the empowerment anger seems to give, must be put in perspective with the possible ultimate cost to my own spirit, and possibly my innocent friends or family, of malice unrelinquished: "See to it that no one misses the grace of God and that no bitter root grows up to cause trouble and defile many" (Heb. 12:15).

There are also difficulties in forgiveness that come from our fears of the process. Some of these fears are closely related to the handling of our anger, so we may have already dealt in part with the resolving of them; for instance, the problem of vulnerability to becoming a victim again or the fear that forgiveness means we now have to "feel good about" a person who has done monstrous wrong.

Beyond these there may also be fear of not being able to stick it out. Forgiveness takes time, may consist of repeated acts of fresh beginnings after new disappointments, and we grow tired of difficult relationships. Already exhausted emotionally by the shock of the wrong done you, there may seem to be no energy left for the long haul of forgiving. There's nothing left in me to give you any more, may be your honest feeling.

Add to this the memory of previous failure in an experiment with forgiving. You tried to forgive a little, back before the record of wrongs mounted up, and you found it very unsatisfying. Nothing seemed better. What will protect you from such discouragement now?

Again, add the fact that the process of forgiveness may require many times of confrontation between culprit and victim. Such confrontation is tricky. Sincerity is hard to measure and you run the risk of being manipulated. On your part, bringing with you even unconscious bitterness will cause your words to quickly become "boiling oil and not the oil of mercy. A cornered creature is remarkably perceptive . . . will sense the hidden attack . . . grow defensive . . . fight the hurt you bring . . . division between you will increase . . ."[11]

What is the use? Would not distance between you, probably permanent distance, be the least hurtful solution?

The answer to these fears must be realistic. Perhaps to admit that what you fear is true may be the best approach. Forgiveness may be a long, long road to travel; there may not be any protection from repeated discouragement and many confrontations may mean trial, error, and frequent failure.

But now comes the grace of God. A large component of that which is created in your spirit by the grace of God is hope. There may be continuing pain, but it can be hopeful pain! Pain that feels like it is part of a birthing labor, and for the hope set before you, you endure that labor pain. God is called "the God of hope" who is able to make us "overflow with hope by the power of the Holy Spirit" (Rom. 15:13).

Key, too, will be your own experience of forgiveness. God's forgiveness of your sins is not only a model for you to copy ("as in Christ God forgave you," Eph. 4:32), but his forgiveness is a source of your power to forgive. Christ crucified and risen is a deep well of water within your life, water for the person thirsty for your forgiveness ("the water I give will become in him a spring of water . . . streams of living water will flow from within him," John 4:14; 7:38).

If you find it hard to forgive, it will help if you think about the other side of the struggle: how hard it may be to receive your forgiveness! And how hard it may be to receive—to truly believe the possibility of God's forgiveness.

The other set of difficulties in forgiveness are in receiving it. The hard-work miracle may be hard to believe as a miracle. Who qualifies for a miracle? Certainly, we think, not a guilty perpetrator of pain in the lives of those whose trust he has betrayed. How can God forgive what *I* have done? Why do I find it so hard to believe that God's mercy can outlast my sinful ugliness?

The answers and solutions may lie in following three steps:

1. Realize the hidden motives you may have in fearing to rest in God's sheer mercy.
2. Remember the tactics of the enemy of your soul's peace and learn how to overcome them.
3. Reexamine the reality and integrity of the forgiveness provided for you in Jesus Christ.

I must also realize that among the factors in my resistance to forgiveness may be a failure to forgive myself. I may be using a refusal to believe God's forgiveness as a mask for self-punishment. There are many shades to this problem which we will examine in more detail in chapter 6. We learn from our parents that wrongdoing deserves punishment, and that became a principle adopted for a lifetime. The need for payment by punishment also grows out of depression and anger with ourselves for having failed to live up to our own expectations. Another habit of the heart is to attempt appeasement: If I punish myself, maybe God will not. Self-punishing sacrifice may be offered in the form of self-denial, self-neglect, or self-hatred.

The idea that everything must be paid for is so deeply ingrained in our thinking. There is "no free lunch." Even forgiveness, apparently free and given in love, must have a catch to it somewhere. The ultimate hidden cost may be more than we are willing or able to pay.

The problem with all this is that my ability to punish myself adequately may run out. With each self-accusing encounter with guilt, payment is made from "a diminishing reserve of dignity and sense of personal worth." Self-dislike and anger against self mounts. Self-punishment is a poor, false, and potentially disastrous substitute for the grace of God!

I also need to realize that a refusal to accept forgiveness can be a form of idolatry and pride. Boldly put, Am I such a unique exception in the world that I can handle my redemption better than God? I would rather do so, perhaps, because the alternative is to accept that I am not the nice person I had thought! I need to hear David's plea in Psalm 32:9, "Do not be like the horse or the mule . . ."

A further step in accepting forgiveness is to remember that Satan is a lying accuser. If my problem is not refusal to acknowledge my sin or a compulsion to be my own judge and jailer, then it may be that I am prey to the accusations of the Evil One as he seeks to keep me from assurance of God's grace.

Scripture calls Satan our "enemy" (adversary), "accuser," and "slanderer" (cf. 1 Tim. 5:14; 1 Peter 5:8; Rev. 12:10). But perhaps he does not accuse us to ourselves as often as he accuses God to us. He seeks to impugn the character of God, so as to discourage us or cause us to doubt. To do this he misrepresents God and God's Word, casting doubt upon God's love, grace, intentions, presence, and forgiveness. The devil always points us away from Christ in his accusations, either to get us to excuse self or dwell upon self. On the other hand, the Holy Spirit points us to Christ, and if he convicts of sin, he also seeks to convince us of grace.

Satan twists Scripture. For example, passages on God's wrath, warning against careless sinners or wicked opponents of the gospel, will be used by Satan to depress or intimidate struggling, fearful Christians. Satan confuses doctrine. For example, he will seek to get us to confuse troubling sin with reigning sin; sin as rebellion in the Christian life with sin reigning in the unbeliever's life. (Romans 6:11–14, "Sin shall not be your master.") How do you meet his accusations?

1. Address the power of sin instead of the shame of sin. Study what it is doing to you more than how it makes you feel. Master the topic in Romans, chapters 5 through 8.
2. Work to keep your conscience clean through confession (Acts 24:16; 1 Tim. 1:19; Heb. 9:14).
3. Fix your eyes upon the evidences of grace in your life, past and present. Search the Scriptures for and meditate upon the promises of grace. "In your temptations run to the promises: they are your Lord's branches hanging over the water, that our Lord's silly, half-drowned children may take a grip of them. . . ." (Samuel Rutherford, writing from exile where he often fought doubts and discouragement).

4. Share your struggle over guilt with another believer and ask them to pray for your assurance of forgiveness.

5. Above all, realize that Satan cannot accuse you, a Christian, before God! God may convict you of sin in order to bring you to confession and cleansing, but he will not listen to the accusations of Satan and change his mind about your salvation! "Who will bring any charge against those whom God has chosen? It is God who justifies. Who is he that condemns? Christ Jesus, who died—more than that, who was raised to life—is at the right hand of God and is also interceding for us" (Rom. 8:33–34).

This brings us to the third step in being able to receive forgiveness: Reexamine the forgiveness provided for you in Jesus Christ to discover again that it is not fragile and conditional.

As in Romans 8, quoted above, in 1 John 2:1 we find a powerful statement about the confidence we may have in God's forgiving of us. "My dear children, I write this to you so that you will not sin. But if anybody does sin, we have one who speaks to the Father in our defense—Jesus Christ, the Righteous One."

Who speaks in your defense? "Jesus Christ, the Righteous One." To whom does he speak in your defense? "The Father." Does the Father need to be begged in your behalf? No, forgiving is the Father's idea from the beginning. There is a holy collusion! "This is love: not that we loved God, but that he loved us and sent his Son as an atoning sacrifice for our sin" (1 John 4:10).

Jesus' *presence* is a continual "speaking." Not as though he has to constantly be there to restrain God, like a kindly older brother who can calm down the temper of an angry parent. No. He is there as God's greatest joy, the Redeemer of the children the Father loves. Justice has been done, evil's doom is sealed, the runaway child has been rescued, and love can celebrate. Jesus, righteous himself, and the answer to the guilt of those who trust him, stands before the throne fully accepted by God. There is courtroom language in this verse, but we must be careful not to impart with our imagination the experiences we may have had in observing human courts. There is no hustle of a busy courtroom and a frazzled judge trying to keep current with an overwhelming caseload. Rather, in your behalf is the great calm of heaven and the continual evidence that sets you free, the presence of the eternal Sacrifice!

5

The Process
of Forgiving Others

Ff forgiveness was as simple as suggested by the common advice to "forgive and forget," there would be no need for a whole chapter on the process of forgiveness. One would simply do it, and it would be completed. But it is not this simple and, as we noted earlier, nor is it this easy.

At the core of forgiveness of another person is releasing the anger that we feel toward them. This is the volitional task, an act of the will. But the preparation for this act of the will involves an emotional task and an intellectual or cognitive one. We can thus describe three stages of the forgiveness process:

1. Preparing to forgive: The emotional work of reexperiencing
2. Beginning to forgive: The cognitive work of reinterpreting
3. Forgiving: The volitional task of releasing

Perhaps, you might say, this makes the business of forgiveness overly complicated. For very simple offenses against us, it is. If someone offends us by an overheard comment, or disappoints us by failing to be sensitive to something we would have expected them to notice, or slights us by some unintentional omission or commission, forgiveness may be as simple as resolving to let go of our hurt and not holding their actions against them. However, in the case of actions which leave emotional wounds which persist over months or years, forgiveness is almost never a matter of simply deciding that it is now time to forgive the other person. Such emotional wounds require healing and the core of that healing is the process of forgiveness, a process that recognizes the nature of our feelings, that reexamines our construal of what happened, and which then releases the anger.

Progress through these stages is seldom direct and linear. Rather we tend to move from stage to stage, often returning to an earlier stage just when we were sure that its work was completed. However, in general we begin the work of forgiveness by dealing with our feelings. After some work at this stage most people notice that they slowly begin to turn to the rethinking of the experience of hurt that is necessary for forgiveness. Only then do they find themselves able to will to forgive in a deep and meaningful way. The stages, while somewhat artificial, do, therefore, seem to approximately describe the journey that most people take on their way to forgiveness.

Preparing for Forgiveness: Reexperiencing the Feelings

The first step in preparing to forgive someone for what they did (or failed to do) is to experience the feelings associated with the hurt which they caused. Before you can forgive the other person you need to be clearly aware of what you are forgiving them for. And this is the reason that for-giveness must start with a focus on the emotional wound.

Reexperiencing the feelings associated with the hurt may sound somewhat strange if you have been experiencing this hurt much of the time since it occurred. If this is the case, you have probably been trying to *not* feel these hurtful feel-ings. And now you are being told to let yourself feel them. But while you may have been experiencing the hurt already, there is a good chance that you have not been facing it head-on. In other words, it is most probable that you have been experiencing it unintentionally and indirectly, not inten-tionally and directly.

The first step in forgiving is facing and examining all the emotions associated with the hurt. As we noted earlier, at the core of every emotional injury is some sense of loss or damage to the self, this being quickly covered by a defen-sive layer of anger. Anger at the one who hurt us keeps the focus on them, rather than us. And for most people this serves them well, as the feelings of pain and loss are gen-erally much more difficult to deal with than those of anger.

If, then, your primary feelings are of anger, it is impor-tant for you to focus on what was taken from you by the hurt. Perhaps you feel some loss of self-esteem or worth. Or perhaps you feel that the hurt took from you your inno-cence or your childhood. Or perhaps it led to a loss of rep-utation or hope for the future. Regardless of what you feel you lost, it is important that you face that loss and allow yourself to mourn it. Without doing so you are much more likely to remain stuck in the anger and be incapable of for-giving the one who hurt you.

If, on the other hand, you are primarily aware of feelings of sadness and loss, this first step in forgiveness is to see if there are any feelings of anger. These feelings may frighten you as you may judge that you should not feel such anger. However, apart from acknowledging them and honestly fac-ing them, forgiveness will be incomplete.

Part of realistically facing our hurt is to name the offense I have suffered. In this I must neither belittle it nor exaggerate it. M. Scott Peck tells us of the need to face the reality of our hurt as he discusses evil in one's own family. "To come to terms with evil in one's parentage is perhaps the most difficult and painful psychological task a human being can be called on to face. Most fail and become its victims. Those who fully succeed in developing the necessary searing vision are those who are able to name it. For to 'come to terms' means to 'arrive at the name.'"[1] Such honest exploration of the past may give great pain but it is the beginning of any true comfort.

If experiencing the feelings is the first step toward forgiveness, expressing them is the second. We are made in such a way that experiences cry out to be shared. Think about the experience of a beautiful sunset. Something within most of us desires the presence of someone with whom we can share such an experience. If no one can experience it firsthand with us, we long to tell someone about it after the fact. This reflects the deep and fundamental social nature of humans. We were created for relationships and it is in these relationships that we fully experience both the pleasures of life and the healing of our wounds.

But there is another reason why the experience of the hurt needs to be shared for it to be healed. Hurts are interpersonal in nature and the instrument of healing must match the instrument of affliction. We were hurt by a person and it is, therefore, in a personal relationship that our healing can be best effected. The hurt begins to be healed as the pain is shared with someone who accepts me and is willing to listen to and accept my expression of hurt and anger.

Because Jesus came to us and suffered with and for us, he understands our suffering and is able to share our burdens. This is his great qualification as our helper when we hurt and need to share our experience with someone. Thus, when we feel ourselves overwhelmed by our hurts, disappointments, or losses, we should remember that Jesus is always available to share these burdens with us. The psalms give many rich examples of people pouring out their pain, anger, doubt, confusion, and hurt to God. God's unconditional acceptance of his children in and through Christ means that he accepts us with whatever struggles we bring to him. And by sharing them with him, we are able to experience and explore things which are often otherwise unbearable.

But sharing experiences with God should not replace sharing them with other humans. God made us in such a way that our needs are not met solely by being in relationship with him. Adam had a perfect unbroken relationship with God. Genesis records that Adam and God regularly walked together in the Garden of Eden and used such times to talk with each other. And yet, in spite of this almost incredible degree of intimate communion with God, God declared that it was not good that Adam was alone! His human nature demanded communion with other humans. He needed to share with another human and not merely with God. And so it is with us.

Sometimes sharing feelings with God is a way to prepare for sharing them with others. But at other times, problems seem more readily shared with other humans and God's love, in these situations, is communicated to us through the love of another person. Concluding that certain hurts cannot be shared as meaningfully with God as with another person is not an indication of a lack of spirituality on my part. Sometimes I may need a listener with a face that I can see or arms with which I can be hugged. But, on the other hand, sometimes my hurts can be uniquely borne by Christ who has suffered in all ways in which I could ever suffer and whom I can, therefore, meet quite uniquely in my own suffering.

Beginning to Forgive: Reinterpreting the Hurt

This emotional work, while necessary and foundational to genuine forgiveness, is still preparatory. It is not yet for-

giveness. Forgiveness does not automatically follow after
such emotional work. In fact, it is quite easy for people to
remain stuck in their painful and angry feelings and be no
better off, no closer to forgiveness.

The beginning of real forgiveness is seeing the one who
hurt you, and the hurtful experience, through new eyes. This
new perspective is essential if you are to release your anger,
not merely express it. And this new perspective involves, in
essence, seeing the person and the situation through God's
eyes. Such a perspective involves three new perceptions: seeing those who hurt me as like me, seeing them as separate
from what they did to me, and seeing myself as like them.

Seeing those who hurt me as like me is seeing them as
they really are. When I do this, I see them as weak and
needy, like me. I also see them as hurting, and possibly as
having hurt me out of their own woundedness. And I may
see them as acting out of self-interest which blinded them
to my needs. If I am honest, I will then have to admit that
they are more like me than I had previously admitted. This
is the first step toward forgiveness.

How can you move from seeing someone as a villain to
seeing them as a person? By praying that God would help
you see them as he does. When you pray this prayer, you
cannot help but begin to see the other person differently.
You may not like what you see and may, consequently, refuse
to look at them through God's eyes of love and compassion.
You may feel that you still need to be angry at them. But forgiveness begins with the willingness to receive help in releasing that anger and the prayer that you may see the other
person as God does is a powerful first step in that direction.

The second result of seeing the other person through
God's eyes is seeing them as separate from what they did
to me. When I look at the one who hurt me through my eyes
of hurt, I see only an object, not a person. But when I look
at them through God's eyes, I see them as a person, not just
what they did to me or do to others.

The third result of seeing the other person through God's eyes is seeing myself as like them. For most of us, this is extremely difficult. Because even if I begin to see the one who hurt me as a person, not simply as the cause of my hurt, I may still see myself as unlike them. I may feel that I am superior to them and that what they did was something that I would never, or could never, do.

In fact, the precise thing which they did may or may not be something I could or would do. Usually we will never know. An old North American Indian saying reminds us to never judge a person until we have walked a mile in their moccasins. In fact, we have not walked in the moccasins of those who hurt us and we can never really know how we would have behaved if we had been born with their genetic makeup and lived through their life experiences.

But whether or not I would have done exactly what they did is not the point. The crucial matter is that I must recognize that I, too, am a person who has hurt others. Intentionally or unintentionally, I have acted out of my neediness and woundedness and have allowed my self-interests to blind me to the interests of others. I, too, have hurt people and have needed their forgiveness. And I, too, have hurt God and needed his forgiveness.

I may have never hurt another by sexually abusing a young child, or by destroying the character of someone by means of slander and lies, or by violating a marriage through adultery. But I am capable of any and all of these acts. And until I can recognize that "there, but for the grace of God, go I," I am incapable of experiencing full and complete healing of the depth of my hurt and I am incapable of forgiving the one who hurt me. When I can allow myself to identify with the person who hurt me by seeing myself to be made of the same basic fabric, then, and only then, will I be able to understand my reaction to them and fully release the anger. Only then will forgiveness be something other than an act of condescension, which is never a satisfactory basis for a genuine release of anger.

As I prepare to move toward a person with forgiveness, I must remember that I am not superior to this other sinner. I may not be exactly like them, but I am more similar to them than to the righteous God! In realizing this, I may be helped by taking time to recall some of my own specific sins against others. I should recall, even if repented of long ago, some of my offenses or acts of neglect against others and think, too, about how I have committed in imagination or desire what I have not done openly.

All this I should do, not to put myself back under the oppression of guilt over sins forgiven, but to feel again a sense of rejoicing gratitude for God's mercy to me and to prepare to forgive "as God in Christ has forgiven me."

If I have never known the experience of having received forgiveness, it is hard to imagine how I could give that gift to anyone else. If, however, in seeing myself as like the person who hurt me, I am able to recall the experience of having been forgiven, I am well on the way to being ready to give that forgiveness myself.

Forgiving: Releasing the Anger

When you get right down to it, forgiveness is really quite simple—it is letting go of your anger and the right to retaliate. There are, however, two important prior steps which, if followed, will increase the chances of success in forgiving another person. These are: understanding the sources of resistance to forgiveness and clarifying misconceptions about it.

Understanding the Sources of Resistance to Forgiveness

Seldom are we ready to release the anger of a significant hurt until we understand why everything within us resists such a step. Forgiveness is often quite impossible when I attempt it solely by means of willpower. Understanding why I resist forgiveness is, therefore, essential if my will is to be free to act. There are many reasons for my natural resistance to forgiveness and these must be acknowledged if they are to be eliminated.

One very frequent reason for resistance to forgiveness is that I may feel it is my right to hold a grudge. In the experience of hurt, my rights were trampled. Now I am going to stand on my rights and it only seems fair to conclude that I have a right to be angry. But accepting anger as a natural response to hurt is not the same as accepting it as a right. Standing on my right to hold a grudge is to stand on dangerous ground. It is to run the risk of chronic bitterness.

Another reason for my resistance to forgiveness is often that I may not yet be ready to give up the sense of power I feel over the person who hurt me. This is best understood by recalling the powerlessness that I experienced in the first stages of hurt. At that point I felt weak, vulnerable, and helpless. But my anger has now restored a sense of power to me and I may be reluctant to give this up.

A related source of resistance may be a reluctance to give up the feelings of moral superiority I now enjoy in relation to the person who hurt me. My wound may have been the occasion for the development of a victim role and I may now be exploiting this role as I nurse a feeling of smug condescension based on moral superiority. Such feelings are often difficult to relinquish.

Sometimes I also resist forgiveness because I equate my nonforgiveness with the punishment of the person who hurt me. It may, in fact, be accurate to conclude that they should be punished. However, the fallacy in this line of reasoning is the assumption that I am the one to do this and that I do so by withholding forgiveness. Vengeance and ultimate justice belong to God. They are his responsibility. Furthermore, while withholding forgiveness does indeed inflict punishment, this punishment is inflicted not on the other but on myself. I must, therefore, give up the idea that it is my responsibility to punish the person who hurt me.

Another reason why I may resist forgiveness is that I may feel I can only forgive the other person if they request it. I may feel that the other person needs to come groveling to me, expressing sorrow and regret for their actions, and offering restitution and promises that they will never hurt me again. But if this was true, we could never forgive a person who was dead and we would be bound to the emotional consequences of hurt for the rest of our lives. Thankfully, this is not the case. My forgiveness of someone is not dependent on any response from them.

A variant of this is that I may feel that I can only forgive the other person if they deserve it. But forgiveness is always undeserved. If someone can do something to earn my forgiveness, they don't need it. Forgiveness has its meaning in the grace of God. There is nothing I can do to earn God's forgiveness and there is nothing another can do to earn mine. Freely we have received, freely we must give.

A final reason for my resistance to forgiveness is that it makes me vulnerable once again. And after the initial hurt, everything within me recoils from taking steps that will lead me toward further vulnerability. This is quite understandable; in fact, it is the most realistic of sources of resistance we have considered. Forgiveness does involve risk and risk involves vulnerability. The major risk of forgiveness is that of further hurt.

But while there are risks to forgiveness, there are also risks to nonforgiveness. And these risks are even greater. The risk of nonforgiveness is that of a life of chronic bitterness and hatred. We noted earlier that this involves the destruction of body, soul, and spirit. The chances of damage to ourselves from withholding forgiveness are extremely high and we must, therefore, be careful to never underestimate these risks. The chances of a subsequent hurt at the hands of the one who hurt me are not to be ignored, but are usually lower than the chances of hurt to myself if I withhold forgiveness. On this basis we would suggest that forgiveness is always the better risk.

Clarifying Misconceptions about Forgiveness

The possibility that I may be able to forgive one who has hurt me will be greatly increased when I remember some things that forgiving is *not.*

Forgiving is not forgetting. To quickly forget a hurt is to repress it and repression does not lead to genuine healing. The emotional pain, the sting of memory, my preoccupation with the wrong done to me, these may fade with time and have less and less emotional energy attached to them. But forgiveness does not eliminate memory. What it does is enable us to control memory, to begin to remember without malice. Rebuilding a relationship may involve creating new, better memories together, but that is different from desperate attempts to "kiss and make up," to hide bad memories under a cover-up of frantically contrived new experiences, a new location, or new possessions.

While I still should expect to be able to remember the hurt after forgiveness, I should also expect that I will be less and less preoccupied with it. In other words, forgiveness should afford me more control over my memory. It should leave me free to recall the hurt if I choose, but also free to not think about it once it comes into consciousness. Memory for the circumstances of the hurt will remain but should, over time, have less and less emotional energy attached to it. Only God can forgive and forget.[2] The rest of us forgive and remember. But through forgiveness, we are able to remember without malice.

Forgiving is not excusing. Seeing the person who hurt me as like me and understanding that we share humanness is not the same as excusing their behavior. There are always reasons why other people behave as they do and sometimes these reasons will even make sense to us if we come to know them. However, reasons and shared human weakness are not the same as excuses. Excuses tend to gloss over the reality of evil, of personal responsibility for wrongs done to another. Indeed, explaining away responsibility for bad behavior is the growing mind-set in our society.

Professor Roger Lundin of Wheaton College tells of the student responses to an essay question on a test he gave. "It asked students to describe the consequences of the fall as John Milton depicts them in Book IX of *Paradise Lost.* Most answers focused upon the discord that entered Adam and Eve's relationship, their shame, and their drastically altered view of God. But several exams contained surprising responses. Each began with a thesis statement something like this: 'The major effect of the fall was to make Adam and Eve change their lifestyle.' What has concerned me over the years has been the inability of many students, when I have related this story to them, to understand the dangers inherent in reducing the expulsion from Eden to a change in lifestyle. A world in which every action manifests nothing more than an individual's flair, his or her peculiar 'style,' is a world in which there is no difference in choosing between gods to worship and ice cream flavors to consume."[3]

If the consequences of wrongs done to us or by us are allowed to become merely problems of lifestyle and the cause of each wrong blamed upon peer pressure or a history of victimization by others, then there is no need for forgiveness because all deeds are excusable. In fact most of what we do to one another in the conflicts of human relationships are inexcusable. Attempts to excuse will block efforts to genuinely forgive and can often turn to bitterness when memory eventually becomes more honest.

Forgiving is not ignoring. I may attempt to ignore the feelings of hurt, or even the person who hurt me, and pretend it did not happen or minimize it in my thinking. A form of this may be my assumption that "time heals all wounds" and try to be patient until my pain goes away or the one who wounded me acknowledges the wrong, repents and approaches me with offered restitution. But to ignore or to overlook wrong is an attempt to change reality by the power of selective memory and will not produce genuine healing.

Forgiving does not require that I offer unconditional trust. In some circumstances I may discern the other person's remorse to be genuine enough to produce changed behavior and, therefore, conclude that I can safely extend complete trust without guarding myself further against recurring hurt. However, in other situations caution is called for. I should not assume that I will never again be hurt in the same way by the same person. Taking steps to minimize that possibility is simply being responsible, to myself and to them. I may genuinely forgive the past and at the same time be cautious around the one who hurt me. Forgiveness is not always incompatible with limited trust.

Forgiveness is hard enough work, though also a miracle, that one does not want to assume the fruitless burden of impossible and disappointing tasks! Actually the prospect of forgiving is lightened considerably by avoiding these misunderstandings.

If these are misunderstandings, what is a realistic understanding of forgiveness? Such an understanding recognizes the following:

> *Forgiveness must be for what people do, not for who they are.* I should forgive people for specific actions, not for character traits. I am not called upon to forgive someone for being selfish or unloving (character traits), but for hurting me with their actions.
>
> *Forgiveness is always done in the midst of confusion.* I will never have all the answers to why the other person did as they did. The past can never be completely reconstructed. It can, however, be redeemed and I can be free of its tyrannizing bondage.

Forgiveness may not heal the relationship. It makes possible reconciliation, but does not produce it. Essentially it is between me and God. If it has beneficial results in terms of the relationship, that's an extra bonus.

Forgiveness may not automatically make me feel better. It is not a magic formula to eliminate pain. It will always be a very important part of the healing of my emotional wounds but this effect may not be instant. I may, therefore, continue to feel anger and hurt even after having forgiven the one who hurt me. I must, therefore, not doubt the genuineness of my forgiveness if after I forgive I continue to feel hurt or anger.

Forgiveness often must be done over and over again. Seldom is it a one time affair. (Remember our discussion of Luke 17:1–10 in chapter 1.) Each subsequent offering of forgiveness renders more complete the former ones. Each act of forgiveness is a giving up of all that I can give up at that time. But over time, I often realize better all there is that I am called to relinquish. Usually, therefore, I am called upon to forgive and to forgive again. With God, forgiveness is complete and we need never ask again for his forgiveness of a previously confessed sin. But our forgiveness is seldom complete the first time.

Forgiveness may take a long time. Because it must often be done over and over again, forgiveness often takes a long time. Forgiving significant hurts sometimes involves a pilgrimage of years, occasionally a lifetime. Some hurts may only be healed completely by the resurrection of the last day! But God wants us to seek healing now, inasmuch as we are in his eyes already raised from death to life spiritually and continual recipients of his enabling grace and power.

Letting Go

The core of forgiveness is letting go of my malice, my right to retaliate, and my right to hang on to the emotional consequences of the hurt. These are the things that I cling to as long as I refuse to forgive. And these are the things, which in forgiveness, I voluntarily choose to relinquish.

In forgiveness I give up the claim I feel I have on the one who hurt me. I consider the account to be balanced. Anything I felt able to hold over the other person, I now relinquish. Forgiveness is not returning evil for evil or insult for insult, but giving a blessing instead. It is wishing the other well; it is praying that God will bless them and facing them in love, not hate. It is giving up my malice.

True forgiveness also involves relinquishing the emotional consequences of the hurt. I may continue to feel anger, hurt, depression, or other such consequences, but I choose to no longer embrace them. They are no longer my right. They are things that I now seek to leave behind me. Recurring waves of anger or pain remind me that healing is not yet complete. However, they are not to be savored in self-pity. Rather, they are to be released as quickly as I am able to do so.

One common consequence of emotional wounds is a tendency to brood on what happened. Forgiving the one who hurt me involves letting go of voluntary brooding over the past. But what am I to do about brooding which seems to be involuntary?

The key to breaking the chain of brooding is to do so at its earliest link. This can often be facilitated by the following:

1. Whenever you begin to recall your loss, take two minutes to think about it (time yourself). The fact of the offense is a sad one and the loss to your peace is real, but you cannot allow yourself to be immobilized by it. Forgiveness can give you more and more control over memory. You are free to recall the hurt if you

choose and also free to not entertain thoughts of it if
it comes into your consciousness.

2. Conclude the two-minute period in prayer to God,
placing your hurt in his hands, asking for help to put
it behind you. Ask for the freedom Jesus promises to
give (John 8:36).

3. Get up and turn to a present chore or responsibility
and pour your energies productively into it. Or, if this
is a period for leisure, concentrate on your enjoyment!
Best of all, turn to the Scriptures, find a passage which
mentions God himself prominently (often this will be
a psalm) and focus on how that portion of majesty of
God and the beauty of his attributes have a way of
shrinking our own size and that of our adversaries into
comforting perspective. (Remember the "think about
these things" passage in Philippians 4:8–9. God himself
is "noble," "right," "pure," "lovely," and "admirable."
And he is the "God of peace" who "will be with you.")

Forgiveness, while never simple, is possible. Never forget this. But also do not forget the fact that the possibility
of forgiveness is grounded not in some quality of you or me
but in the character and actions of God. My ability to forgive those who hurt me is based on the healing grace of
God, his forgiveness of me, his grace in the lives of other
humans who have forgiven me in the past, and his grace in
me which now makes possible my taking the first steps toward forgiveness of the one who has hurt me.

Grasping firmly onto this grace is also the key to forgiving ourselves. It is to this challenge that we now turn in the
next chapter.

6

The Challenge
of Forgiving Ourselves

As hard as it is to forgive another person, many people find it even more difficult to forgive themselves. Often these same people find it equally hard to accept forgiveness from another. Such inability to receive forgiveness is as destructive to body, soul, and spirit as a failure to give it. It is important, therefore, that we understand both why receiving forgiveness often seems impossible and the liberating possibilities for self-forgiveness that reside in the uniquely Christian concept of grace. This will be the focus of this final chapter.

The Tyranny of Guilt

The inability to forgive oneself and the unwillingness to receive the forgiveness of another both reflect the same underlying core of guilt. Whereas an inability to give forgiveness to another person usually has at its core unresolved anger, an inability to receive forgiveness is based on unresolved guilt. It is important, therefore, that we clearly understand this concept of guilt.

Guilt may well be the most painful human emotion. Think of the pain and anguish that you would feel if you backed your car out of a driveway and ran over and killed your child. Who could fail to understand the self-recrimination a parent would experience under such circumstances. Everything within you would cry out for the chance to live that moment over again, this time taking more care. And knowing that this was impossible, everything within you would ache with the pain you inflicted on your child and which you now wish you could bear for him or her.

A current high profile murder case in Toronto highlights such guilt on the part of parents. A sixteen-year-old girl was abducted, raped, and murdered after being locked out of the house by her parents because she failed to return home by the agreed upon curfew. Imagine the guilt experienced by those parents. The horror of losing their daughter in such a way is compounded by their overwhelming guilt at having contributed to her vulnerability by locking her out of the house. The torment experienced by these parents is almost unimaginable.

Guilt feelings are a complex combination of painful inner emotions. Dr. Bruce Narramore suggests that guilt can be understood as self-inflicted punishment that usually results in shame or a loss of self-esteem and feelings of isolation or rejection.[1] The core of self-inflicted punishment is reflected in statements such as "I just wish I could die," or "I just feel like kicking myself." Shame and self-disgust are expressed in statements such as "I just hate myself," or "I'm disgusted with myself," and feelings of isolation or rejection are revealed by such statements as "I just want to run away and never have to face anybody again" or, "If you really knew me you would be disgusted too." When these feelings combine in the unique way in which they do in guilt, the result is an almost overwhelming feeling of self-loathing.

While this describes the inner experience of guilt, each person's response to that guilt is unique. One person may be mobilized to quick rectification of the situation or, if the situation cannot be rectified, to some symbolic actions which suggest rectification. On the other hand, another person may be immobilized by the inner pain. Some people may appear to feel virtually nothing at all but may express their guilt through self-destructive behavior. And while some remain stuck in forms of self-punishment, others wallow in shame and feelings of inferiority and self-disgust.

In summary, guilt is the name we give to the complicated psychological reaction we normally experience in response to disparity between who we are and who we think we ought to be. This reaction varies considerably among people but usually includes self-punishment, self-hatred, and a sense of shame or inferiority.

Is Guilt the Voice of God?

Guilt is hard enough to ignore if it is simply a painful feeling. However, it is even harder to deal with if we conclude that guilt is God's means of speaking to us. Many Christians equate guilt feelings and divine conviction of sin. They view feelings of guilt as God's way of getting our attention and motivating us to change our behavior.

A television evangelist was recently heard to say that "guilt is God's way of making us want to repent from sin so that he can forgive us and make us guilt-free." Apart from the absurdity of the notion of God making us feel guilt so that he can remove those feelings of guilt, this sort of understanding appears to be quite common among Christians. Somehow we think that the painful feelings of guilt must be from God, a little dose of punishment for our sins so that we will turn to him and escape further, more serious punishment.

This view of guilt is also reflected in the fact that some Christians equate guilt and spirituality. In such a view, the worse a person feels about themselves, the more spiritually mature they are judged to be. Low self-esteem is thought to be both an antidote to pride and a measure of humility. So, if feeling badly about oneself is a mark of spirituality, focusing on one's guilt is a dependable means to achieve such a spiritual goal.

If we think that God uses guilt to make us do what he wants us to do, we are also more likely to employ guilt motivation ourselves. This is, in part, why such use of guilt in the manipulation of others is so common in some Christian circles. Whether in preaching, parenting, or other relationships, guilt is stirred up with the intent that the other person will do what we think they should do. And we feel justified in using such blatant forms of emotional manipulation because we think God uses the same tactics.

But does he? The answer is an emphatic NO! There is no biblical evidence of God using guilt to motivate people. The Christian God is in the business of removing guilt, not producing it.

Perhaps the clearest indication of God's avoidance of guilt manipulation is found in the story of the fall in Genesis 3. There we are told that Adam and Eve, having eaten of the forbidden fruit, felt shame, discovered their nakedness and were uncomfortable in this condition. They also felt a desire to run and hide from God. His presence, so they thought, would make them feel even worse. And so, when he came to walk with them in the cool of the day, they hid. Furthermore, they attempted to deal with their shame by covering themselves with leaves. And what did God do? Did he berate them and humiliate them in order to make them feel even worse than they already did? No. He intervened in grace to minimize the consequences of guilt. Rather than stripping them of their crude leaf garments and rubbing their noses in their shame, he gently and graciously prepared for them new, better clothing so that they would not need to experience the destructive effects of guilt.

God saw the guilt of Adam and Even and sought to remove it, not intensify it. He wasn't primarily interested in helping them learn some lesson from it. He desired a restoration of a broken relationship and reached out in love, not condemnation.

Scriptures give absolutely no support for the notion that guilt, or any other form of self-hatred or inner punishment, is a constructive motivation. Self-loathing does not honor God. Scriptures affirm our worth, not our worthlessness. Creation, the incarnation, and redemption all affirm the immense worth of humans, even humans who have fallen into sin.

In point of fact, feelings of guilt do not make us better people. Guilt is a tremendously destructive emotion. It really has no redeeming quality. Guilt reduces self-esteem and feelings of well-being; it impairs our emotional availability to others and our capacity for love; it restricts our capacity for work, play, problem-solving, and creativity; it increases our self-preoccupation and self-encapsulation; it blocks our sensitivity and response to both God and other people; and it increases hostility, anxiety, and depression.

The Christian response to sin is repentance, not guilt. Guilt is essentially a self-punishment, a way of attempting to atone for one's own sins. As such, whether we realize it or not, guilt is a way of saying, "Christ's death and God's forgiveness are not sufficient to take care of my sins. That may work for the sins of others but I will pay for my own sins by inflicting some inner psychic pain upon myself." Once seen in this light, we see that guilt involves both moral masochism ("I will pay for this myself") and pride ("I don't deserve to be forgiven; I deserve to be punished"). Others may deserve to receive God's forgiveness and his work of atonement for their sins, but I am so special that I deserve something else.

Guilt immobilizes more often than it leads to changed behavior. Judas is a good example of the destructive nature of guilt. After his betrayal of Jesus he sought not forgiveness, but punishment. He went out and hanged himself. In contrast, Peter responded to his betrayal of Jesus very differently. He wept in repentance and chose to accept the forgiveness of his Lord. Repentance is a love-motivated desire to change, rooted in concern for the offended person and one's relationship to God. Guilt, on the other hand, is essentially a self-punitive strategy to attempt to atone for one's own sins.

Grace: The Only Solution to Guilt

If guilt produces bondage and makes it difficult to receive forgiveness, either from ourselves or others, grace is the radical answer to guilt and the only route to freedom from its tyranny. Guilt has its foundation in works-righteousness. The psychology of guilt is the psychology of self-justification, of effort to get our act together and to get our house in order. Guilt is learned in the context of conditional love, encountered in relationships with parents and significant others who lead us to believe that our worth is dependent upon our performance.

But true Christianity is diametrically opposed to such conditional worth and efforts to deserve love. God says to us "YOU ARE OF SUPREME WORTH BECAUSE I MADE YOU IN MY IMAGE. AS A RESULT OF YOUR SIN, YOU DESERVE DEATH AND HAVE NO WAY OF EARNING MY FAVOR. BUT, I FREELY, GRACIOUSLY, EXTRAVAGANTLY, AND EVEN RECKLESSLY EXTEND MY FAVOR TO YOU. I ACCEPT YOU! JUST AS YOU ARE! AS A SINNER!"

The radical message of Christianity is that in grace, God accepts us, blots out our conscious guilt feelings, and then brings to consciousness and heals our deeper repressed guilt. All this is based on our being accepted in him.

Such grace is totally alien to human psychology. It is inherently at cross purposes with the drive of our own spirits to self-justification.

Left to ourselves, none of us would ever catch the idea, to say nothing about our bent to think of it as erroneous and impossible. If the idea of grace were not delivered to us with authority, and if it were not so immediately and obviously the thing that changes our lives redemptively—both psychologically and spiritually—we would tolerate nothing of it. The notion of grace as the unconditional, universal, and total divine acceptance of all of us is inherently at crosswinds with the drive of our own spirits to self-certification and to the achievement of personality, stability and meaning. It is the theology of grace which . . . is the one thing that can radically change human nature . . . The theology of grace is the most healing intervention ever undertaken for the population of this planet.[2]

God accepts us as and where we are for the sake of what and who we can become. He comes with forgiveness and we dishonor him when we refuse that forgiveness.

In summary, guilt is a destructive, neurotic effort at self-justification that has no place in Christianity. Repentance, on the other hand, is crucial if we are to be made whole. Repentance is a healing response to our sin that recognizes our need of God and turns to him for help and forgiveness. Receipt of divine grace and recognition of the fact that we are accepted in Christ is what makes this possible. This is the good news—the gospel!

Richard Ecker notes that as a clergyman he has talked with a lot of hurting people over the years. With few exceptions, they were all solidly in touch with the extent of their sins; where they needed help was getting in touch with the grace of God. He then states, "If I had to specify the most fundamental deficiency in emotional dysfunction, it would be the inability to experience the unconditional. To the emotionally disabled, grace—unconditional love—is a totally foreign concept, at least at the gut level where it counts. This is because their personalities have been shaped so totally by programming that makes value conditional."[3]

We all desperately need to be solidly in touch with the good news of God's grace. But everything within us runs from this. We want to get our house in order and then let God love and accept us. This is the psychology of works-righteousness. And its fruit is guilt.

How to Forgive Yourself

Have you done something that feels so awful that you have concluded that you do not deserve forgiveness? Perhaps you have violated someone's trust. Or possibly you did what you have publicly preached against. Perhaps, you have broken God's moral law, and have also broken your own moral standards. Consequently you are disappointed in yourself. Deeply disappointed. Possibly shocked. And you have concluded that you do not deserve forgiveness.

You are right about that. You don't deserve forgiveness. If you did, you wouldn't need it. That's the whole point of forgiveness. But while you do not deserve it, you need it. Guilt and other forms of self-punishment do not, and cannot, atone for what you have done. Only God's forgiveness can. If he can forgive you, how dare you not forgive yourself!

Forgiving yourself, while never simple, involves three things: repenting of my pride, repenting of my efforts at self-justification, and accepting God's forgiveness.

1. *Repenting of my pride:* Pride is ultimately a refusal to accept my place. The root of pride was seen in the Garden of Eden when Adam and Eve, not content with their lot as humans desired to be like God and know good and evil. Repenting of my pride means accepting myself as a frail and imperfect human. It means seeing myself realistically—as one who is imperfect and sinful, who hurts others and myself, and who, therefore, needs the forgiveness of self, others, and God. It involves accepting myself as I am. This is not the same as complacency and is not incompatible with a desire to change and grow. But the starting point of my growth is accepting myself as I am. Just as God does.

2. *Repenting of my efforts at self-justification:* The second step in forgiving myself is taking my hands off the controls of justification and letting myself be healed by God's gracious forgiveness. This requires that I recognize that being acceptable does not depend upon my character or behavior but upon God's character. This is the lesson of the parable of the prodigal son (Luke 15:11–32), a parable we examined in chapter 3. Both the younger and older sons had to learn that sonship does not hinge upon the character of the son but on the character of the father. Measuring up is not the issue in Yahweh's universe. Neither is our guilt or our sin. The issue is God's grace.

3. *Accepting God's forgiveness of me:* Micah, the prophet, declared that God has cast all our sins into the depths of the sea (Micah 7:18–20). If this is true, they are erased! Gone! As completely as if they had never existed! They can never be recovered or resurrected to be used against us again!

Forgiving myself is acknowledging that if God says my sins are gone, then they are gone. If he says that they are erased from the record of his memory, it is letting go of them from mine. As we noted earlier, I may not forget them. But, if I have accepted God's forgiveness, I will no longer hold those sins against me.

Implications of Living in Grace

We have already acknowledged that it is hard to live in grace. Often other Christians make it hard. But the only alternative to grace is guilt. If then, I am to be free of guilt and live in grace, how will I live?

1. I will be realistic in my expectations of both myself and others. I will not be surprised by my failures and

sin. Although both will disappoint me, neither will shock me. Nor will they shock me when I encounter them in others.

2. I will be slow to feel anger or guilt and will let go of both quickly. I will keep short accounts with these destructive emotions. Recognizing and dealing with them quickly, I will release them and seek to give or receive forgiveness as soon as possible.

3. I will be ready to treat others as God treats me. My relationships with others will be characterized by extravagant generosity, unconditional acceptance, deep respect, and seeing the other for who they can become rather than what they now appear to be.

4. I will be ready to attempt the hard work of reconciliation with those whom I have hurt or by whom I have been hurt.

5. I will be ready to become an agent of reconciliation in a world of broken people, relationships, and communities.

Grace heals. Guilt and anger bring bondage. Forgiveness of myself or of others is a gift of grace. Ultimately, both are made possible by the experience of having been forgiven. As I see myself as one who in the past, present, and future has, been, is, and will be in need of forgiveness, and as I see myself as having received that forgiveness from God and possibly others, I am then able to offer that same forgiveness to others and even to myself. But, none of this would be possible if God had not introduced forgiveness into the equation. He is the one who has broken for all time the cycle of works, effort, failure, and punishment. His gift to us is the gift of grace. May we live in this grace and offer this same gift to those with whom we have contact.

Notes

Chapter 1: The Importance of Forgiveness

1. Philip Yancey, *Disappointment with God* (Grand Rapids: Zondervan, 1988).

2. Dennis and Matthew Linn, *Healing Life's Hurts: Healing Memories Through the Five Stages of Forgiveness* (New York: Paulist, 1979), p. 151.

3. R. Lofton Hudson, *Grace is Not a Blue-Eyed Blond* (Waco, Texas: Word, 1972), p. 72, quoted in *Forgiveness*, Dan Hamilton (Downers Grove: InterVarsity Press, 1980), p. 6.

4. Whereas Genesis 50:26 reminds us of Genesis 3:19, the first judgment on sin, Genesis 50:15–21 reminds us of Genesis 3:15, the first promise of salvation.

5. Lyman T. Lundeen, "Forgiveness and Human Relationships," in *Counseling and the Human Predicament*, ed. by LeRoy Aden and David G. Benner (Grand Rapids: Baker Book House, 1989), p. 186.

6. Ibid., pp. 191–92.

Chapter 2: The Possibility of Forgiveness

1. G. C. Berkhouwer, *Sin* (Grand Rapids: Wm. B. Eerdmans Publishing Co., 1971), p. 387.

2. Ibid., p. 392.

3. Walter Wangerin Jr., *As For Me and My House* (Nashville: Thomas Nelson Publishers, 1990), pp. 90–91.

4. Ibid.

Chapter 3: The Necessity of Forgiveness

1. Editorial, *The New Yorker Magazine*, January 29, 1990, p. 25.

2. Ibid.

3. Dennis Guernsey, *Sometimes It's Hard to Love God* (Downers Grove: InterVarsity Press, 1989), pp. 142–43.

4. William G. Justice, Jr., *Guilt and Forgiveness* (Grand Rapids: Baker Book House, 1980), p. 91.

5. See pages 44–49 of David G. Benner, *Healing Emotional Wounds* (Grand Rapids: Baker Book House, 1990) for further discussion of these masks of anger.

6. Lyman T. Lundeen, *Counseling and the Human Predicament*, ed. Leroy Aden and David G. Benner (Grand Rapids: Baker Book House, 1989), p. 181.

7. Lewis B. Smedes, *Forgive and Forget* (San Francisco: Harper and Row, 1984), pp. 106–7, 113.

8. S. Bruce Narramore, "Guilt: Where Theology and Psychology Meet," in *Wholeness and Holiness*, ed. H. Newton Malony (Grand Rapids: Baker Book House, 1983), p. 134.

Chapter 4: The Difficulty of Forgiveness

1. John Goldingay, *Songs from a Strange Land* (Downers Grove: InterVarsity Press, 1978), pp. 162–63.

2. Lewis B. Smedes, *Forgive and Forget* (New York: Simon and Schuster, 1984), pp. 141–42.

3. Lyman T. Lundeen, *Counseling and the Human Predicament*, ed. Leroy Aden and David G. Benner (Grand Rapids: Baker Book House, 1989), pp. 178–80.

4. Richard P. Lord, "Do I Have to Forgive?" *The Christian Century* (October 9, 1991), pp. 902–3.

5. Leon Morris, *The Atonement* (Downers Grove: InterVarsity Press, 1983), pp. 199–200.

6. For more on this and other sources of resistance to forgiveness, see chapter 5 of David G. Benner, *Healing Emotional Wounds*, pp. 113–17.

7. Lyman T. Lundeen, *Counseling and the Human Predicament*, ed. Leroy Aden and David G. Benner (Grand Rapids: Baker Book House, 1989), pp. 190–91.

8. Wangerin, p. 81.

9. Rinda G. Rogers, "Forgiveness and the Healing of the Family," in *Counseling and the Human Predicament*, ed. Leroy Aden and David G. Benner (Grand Rapids: Baker Book House, 1989), pp. 198–200.

10. Dan Hamilton, *Forgiveness* (Downers Grove, InterVarsity Press, 1980) pp. 22–23.

11. Walter Wangerin Jr., *As For Me and My House* (Nashville: Thomas Nelson Publishers, 1990), p. 100.

Chapter 5: The Process of Forgiving Others

1. M. Scott Peck, *The People of the Lie*, quoted in *From Fear to Freedom*, Rose Marie Miller (Wheaton: Harold Shaw Publishers, 1994), p. 85.

2. In God's forgiving of our sins he tells us that he "remembers" our sins "no more" (Jer. 31:34; Heb. 8:12; 10:17). Since we are to forgive as we have been forgiven, is it then expected of us to literally forget the hurts done to us? The answer

to this is found in the kind of "forgetting" exercised by God himself. He is omniscient, knowing all things possible at all times and at every moment in time. God cannot forget our sins in the sense that he loses them from his memory. By forgetting, he must mean that he sets aside the punishment we deserve when he forgives us. He holds the guilt of our sins over our heads no longer. Our past culpability is not a factor in how he treats us in the future—except to continue his forgiving, healing mercy. Our "forgetting" of the offenses done to us means that we will not in the future "use" the offense as a reason to punish the offender. We will not raise it as an issue between us nor use it as a weapon against the other person. We will not continually remind third parties about it. And we will determine to work at not dwelling upon it in our own minds. This is the biblical sense in which we might speak of "forgiving and forgetting."

3. Roger Lundin, "The Ultimately Liveral Condition," *First Things*, April 1995, p. 25.

Chapter 6: The Challenge of Forgiving Ourselves

1. S. Bruce Narramore, *No Condemnation* (Grand Rapids: Zondervan, 1984), p. 27.

2. J. Harold Ellens, *God's Grace and Human Health* (Abingdon, 1982), p. 67.

3. Richard E. Ecker, "Whatever Happened to Grace?" *Perspectives* (March 1992, vol. 7, number 3), p. 14.